Red Rocks Climbing

SUPERTOPOS

Red Rocks Climbing
SUPERTOPOS

Greg Barnes
Larry DeAngelo

Published by
SuperTopo
2 Bradford Way
Mill Valley, CA 94941
www.supertopo.com

Topos and text by Greg Barnes
History by Larry DeAngelo
Managing Editor and Designer: Sarah Felchlin
Contributing Designer: David Safanda
Publisher: Chris McNamara

Front cover: Dan McQuade on the aesthetic Graveyard Waltz (5.12). *Photo by Greg Epperson*
Frontispiece: Dan McQuade on Pitch 4 of Cloud Tower. *Photo by Greg Epperson.*
Back cover: Meryl Singer floats up The Gift (5.12c) at The Gallery. *Photo by Jim Thornburg.*

Library of Congress Cataloging-in-Publication Data

Barnes, Greg, 1971-
  Red Rocks climbing : SuperTopos / by Greg Barnes.-- 1st ed.
    p. cm.
  ISBN 0-9672391-6-8
  1. Rock climbing--Nevada--Red Rock Canyon National Conservation
Area--Guidebooks. 2. Red Rock Canyon National Conservation Area
(Nev.)--Guidebooks. I. Title.
GV199.42.N32 R433 2004
796.52'23'0979313--dc22
                                        2003025298
Printed in Canada

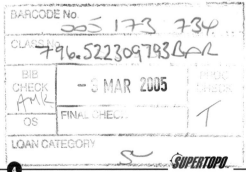

Contents

Warning!

Climbing is an inherently dangerous sport in which severe injuries or death may occur. Relying on the information in this book may increase the danger.

When climbing you can only rely on your skill, training, experience, and conditioning. **If you have any doubts as to your ability to safely climb any route in this guide, do not try it.**

This book is neither a professional climbing instructor nor a substitute for one. **It is not an instructional book. Do not use it as one.** It contains information that is nothing more than a compilation of opinions about climbing in Red Rocks. **These opinions are neither facts nor promises.** Treat the information as opinions and nothing more. Do not substitute these opinions for your own common sense and experience.

Assumption of Risk

There may be errors in this book resulting from the mistakes of the authors and/or the people with whom they consulted. The information was gathered from a variety of sources, which may not have been independently verified. Those who provided the information may have made mistakes in their descriptions. The authors may have made mistakes in their conveyance of the information in this book. **The authors cannot, therefore, guarantee the correctness of any of the information contained in this book.** The topographical maps, photo-diagrams, difficulty ratings, protection ratings, approach and/or descent information, suggestions about equipment, and other matters may be incorrect or misleading. Fixed protection may be absent, unreliable, or misplaced. **You must keep in mind that the information in this book may be erroneous, so use your own judgement when choosing, approaching, climbing, or descending from a route described in this book.**

DO NOT USE THIS BOOK UNLESS YOU [AND YOUR ESTATE] PROMISE NEVER TO TRY TO SUE US IF YOU GET HURT OR KILLED.

Disclaimer of Warranties

THE AUTHORS AND PUBLISHER WARN THAT THIS BOOK CONTAINS ONLY THE AUTHORS' OPINIONS ON THE SUBJECTS DISCUSSED. THEY MAKE NO OTHER WARRANTIES, EXPRESSED OR IMPLIED, OF MERCHANTABILITY, FITNESS FOR PURPOSE, OR OTHERWISE, AND IN ANY EVENT, THEIR LIABILITY FOR BREACH OF ANY WARRANTY OR CONTRACT WITH RESPECT TO THE CONTENT OF THIS BOOK IS LIMITED TO THE PURCHASE PRICE OF THE BOOK. THEY FURTHER LIMIT TO SUCH PURCHASE PRICE THEIR LIABILITY ON ACCOUNT OF ANY KIND OF NEGLIGENT BEHAVIOR WHATSOEVER ON THEIR PART WITH RESPECT TO THE CONTENTS OF THIS BOOK.

Acknowledgements

First, a BIG thanks to all the climbers—folks like George and Joanne Urioste, Joe Herbst, Randy Grandstaff, Mike Ward, Mike Clifford, and many others—who spent so much time and effort establishing all the great Red Rocks climbs. We often take routes for granted, but without the pioneering efforts of climbers going into uncharted vertical terrain, risking loose rock and the truly unknown, there wouldn't be rock climbing as we know it.

SuperTopo is a team of climbers who are equally motivated to avoid real jobs, climb a lot, and as a result, be poor. Sarah Felchlin is the Managing Editor and Designer and organizes the production of each book. Greg Barnes is our top author who has endless Red Rocks climbing beta permanently wired into his head. Randy Spurrier is the force behind the SuperTopo web site. Larry DeAngelo is the SuperTopo Red Rocks historian. David Safanda is a pro designer who helps keep SuperTopo looking slick. Chris McNamara is the publisher who spends way more time thinking about guidebooks than anyone should.

Thanks to those helping replace old bolts all around Red Rocks: Dan McQuade, Mike White, Jack Hoeflich, Mark Limage, George Urioste, Lawrence Garcia, Karin Wuhrmann, Matt Schutz, Rick Podetke, Gary Fike, Laura Snider, Barry Hutten, and too many others to name.

Thanks to Jed Botsford and Patrick Putnam for being responsible and friendly links between the climbing community and the land managers, and to all those involved with the Las Vegas Climbers Liaison Council. Thank you to Bruce Bindner for the Crimson Chrysalis topo. A special thanks to Gene Malone for helping copyedit the book.

Thank you to all of the people who emailed in feedback: Andrew Barnes, Adrian Burke, Trevor Jones, Ken Klis, Rapahel Lagrange, Jeff Larsen, Richard Kim Miller, Cherie Moulin, Jonathan Peischl, Joe Ramos, William Segal, Rafael de Santiago, Florence Scholl, and Xavier Wasiak.

And a huge thanks to everyone out there in the climbing community. I want to say thanks to my many partners, to the great folks I run into climbing all over the place, and to all the people who fight to keep access open for rock climbing in an overly litigious society. I think we often don't think about just how friendly, supportive, and interesting climbers are as a group. Thanks to the whole climbing community for just being downright fun to hang out with.

– Greg Barnes

ACCESS: It's every climber's concern

The Access Fund, a national, non-profit climbers' organization, works to keep climbing areas open and to conserve the climbing environment. Need help with closures? Land acquisition? Legal or land management issues? Funding for trails and other projects? Starting a local climbers' group? CALL US!

Climbers can help preserve access by being committed to leaving the environment in its natural state. Here are some simple guidelines:

• **ASPIRE TO CLIMB WITHOUT LEAVING A TRACE,** especially in environmentally sensitive areas like caves. Chalk can make a significant impact on dark and porous rock—don't use it around historic rock art. Pick up litter, and leave trees and plants intact.

• **DISPOSE OF HUMAN WASTE PROPERLY.** Use toilets whenever possible. If toilets are not available, dig a "cat hole" at least six inches deep and 200 feet from any water, trails, campsites, or the base of climbs. *Always pack out toilet paper.* On big wall routes, use a "poop tube" and carry waste up and off with you (the old "bag toss" is now illegal in many areas).

• **USE EXISTING TRAILS.** Cutting across switchbacks causes erosion. When walking off-trail, tread lightly, especially in the desert where cryptogamic soils (usually a dark crust) take thousands of years to form and are easily damaged. Be aware that "rim ecologies" (the clifftop) are often highly sensitive to disturbance.

• **BE DISCREET WITH FIXED ANCHORS.** *Bolts are controversial and are not a convenience—don't place them unless they are really necessary.* Camouflage all anchors. Remove unsightly slings from rappel stations (better to use steel chain or welded cold shuts). Bolts sometimes can be used proactively to protect fragile resources—consult with your local land manager.

• **RESPECT THE RULES** and speak up when other climbers don't. Expect restrictions in designated wilderness areas, rock art sites, caves, and in sensitive wildlife areas such as nesting sites for birds of prey. *Power drills are illegal in wilderness areas and all national parks.*

• **PARK AND CAMP IN DESIGNATED AREAS.** Some climbing areas require a permit for overnight camping.

• **MAINTAIN A LOW PROFILE.** Leave the boom box and day-glo clothing at home. The less climbers are seen and heard, the better.

• **RESPECT PRIVATE PROPERTY.** Be courteous to land owners. Don't climb where you're not wanted.

• **JOIN THE ACCESS FUND.** To become a member, make a tax-deductible donation of $25.

THE ACCESS FUND
Keeping climbing areas open and conserving the climbing environment
P.O. Box 17010
Boulder, CO 80308

A deadly bolt more than 20 years old ... one of several
thousand on popular climbs throughout the United States.

A new bolt rated to over 5,000 pounds. The ASCA
wants to replace the bad bolt above with one of these.

Bad Bolts Kill

We need YOUR help. The American Safe Climbing Association has helped replace more
than 4,500 bolts throughout the country and almost 500 in Red Rocks alone. We estimate that
there are more than 20,000 bad bolts remaining on popular climbs today. Your $50 donation
will make at least one route safe . . . and that one route could be the next one you climb. The
ASCA would like to get there before you do.

Does your crag need
re-bolting? Please
contact us.

asca
American Safe Climbing Association

❏ $25 Supporter   ❏ $50 Contributor   ❏ $100 Advocate   ❏ $500 Lifer

Name _____
Address _____

E-Mail/Phone _____

All contributors receive the ASCA newsletter.
Make checks payable to: ASCA, 2 Bradford Way, Mill Valley, CA 94941
or donate online at www.safeclimbing.org

The American Safe Climbing Association is a 501(c)3 organization and contributions are tax-deductible.

Introduction

by Greg Barnes

With steep, moderate routes, cracks that eat up pro, and tightly bolted face pitches, many long routes at Red Rocks give you high adventure without the runouts so common in many areas. Varnished edges, incut jugs, splitter cracks, technical faces, fun chimneys—Red Rocks multi-pitch routes have it all. Bolted anchors on many popular routes quicken the pace and allow easy retreat. Red Rocks multi-pitch climbs are just downright fun, but that's only half the story. Red Rocks also has tons of shorter routes, great sport climbs, and excellent bouldering. The canyons of Red Rocks are blissfully free of traffic noise and the reminders of civilization, and Desert Bighorn easily outnumber hikers. As you get back in the canyons, you realize the awesome scale of the 3,000-foot sandstone escarpment, and how even the very long routes rarely tackle more than half of a wall's relief. During the daytime, Las Vegas thankfully remains hidden away, and only at night, with the glow of casinos on the skyline, do you realize just how close Red Rocks is to Sin City.

Yet the huge and rapidly expanding Las Vegas, if not one of the attractions, is one of the main conveniences of climbing at Red Rocks. Cheap airfare, endless neon nightlife, restaurants, coffee shops, supermarkets, libraries, and the infamous Strip—are all only a few minutes away.

Even more convenient than the city is the plethora of sport climbing, bouldering, and short trad routes that bring many climbers to Red Rocks in the first place. And with the development of hundreds of sport routes on the limestone cliffs in the area, climbers are no longer limited to the often overcrowded, but excellent, sport crags at the start of the Red Rocks Loop Road. These limestone cliffs are often at higher elevations, and offer great alternatives for warmer days.

All told, the classics of Red Rocks are uniquely accessible, often relatively low on the commitment scale, and undeniably high on the pure climbing fun scale! Here we give you SuperTopo guides of some of Red Rocks' best—including a few never before published routes.

Red Rocks Historical Overview

Prior to 1970, climbing in Red Rocks was a low-key affair. To the extent that technical climbing was being done, it was mostly in the category of general mountaineering. The practitioners were a group of climbers usually referred to as the "Sierra Club" set. (This goes all the way back to a time when the Sierra Club focused on leading outdoor activities.) The routes of this era were typically unrecorded "class 4" operations that linked ledge systems and broken areas to find their way up the walls and to the summits. Climbers such as Howard Booth, Vern Bostick, and Jeff Lansing navigated the canyons and cliffs in these early explorations. One eager participant was local teenager Joe Herbst.

Joe spent the summer of 1970 working for the Palisade School of Mountaineering in the company of luminaries such as Don Jensen and Doug Robinson. Following an autumn in Yosemite, Joe returned home to Las Vegas prepared for great things. Over the next decade he pioneered first ascents of innumerable Red Rocks classics from short crag testpieces, to long free routes, to big aid walls. His pure clean climbing ethic, strongly influenced by Doug Robinson, in turn influenced an emerging generation of local climbers who followed him.

By the late 1970s, George and Joanne Urioste were beginning to make themselves noticed in the local climbing scene. With a good eye for the beautiful line, and a willingness to work very hard on long bolted stretches, the Uriostes initiated a new era in Red Rocks climbing. Drawing from a knowledge of their own routes, and with much reference to Joe Herbst's notebook,

Tori Allen on Caustic (5.11b). (Greg Epperson)

Joanne Urioste authored the original Red Rocks climbing guide in 1984. The ensuing surge in popularity propelled Red Rocks to world-class status as a rock climbing destination.

– Larry DeAngelo

Welcome to Red Rocks Climbing

Our goal in this guidebook is to provide you with everything a climber needs to know about Red Rocks' finest climbing routes—including our namesake SuperTopo—in order to prepare you for an awesome climbing adventure. We chose these routes because of their exceptional rock quality, elegant lines, and outstanding views.

Many of these routes played a historic role in the development of Red Rocks climbing. As we do in all of our SuperTopo guidebooks, we've taken the time to provide you with the history for each route as well as the climbing info. If you're like us you'll find the experience of climbing these classic routes enhanced by the rich history and stories of the colorful characters that first pioneered the climbs.

We hope you enjoy climbing these routes as much as we do. You can be assured that they will offer a superb experience.

About the Crags

East Face Windy Peak (5.6-5.9)
The East Face of Windy Peak has great short trad routes with less crowds.

Whiskey Peak (5.9-5.11c)
The middle section of Whiskey Peak is home to some of Red Rocks' best splitter cracks and some excellent face climbs.

Lotta Balls Wall and Alcohol Wall (5.7-5.10b)
The Lotta Balls area is full of clean cracks and dihedrals that form steep, moderate climbs on excellent dark brown rock.

East Face of Mescalito (5.9-5.10b)
This face has great steep climbing on somewhat runout routes, with morning sun and afternoon shade, and close proximity to several other two- to four-pitch routes and the Brass Wall.

Brass Wall (5.6-5.10d)
Quality cracks, a short approach, and a good concentration of moderate climbs make the Brass Wall one of the most popular traditional crags at Red Rocks.

Ragged Edges, Hidden Falls Wall, and Case Face (5.5-5.12d)
Only a few hundred yards from the road, these great climbs are popular when the weather is appropriate since the walls only get morning sun.

The Gallery (5.8-5.12c)
These short, juggy, and steep sport climbs are in a great sunny location—the most popular sport climbing spot in Red Rocks.

Magic Bus (5.8-5.9)
Great sunny crag with a few well-protected climbs, both sport and trad.

About the Climbs

Here is a brief summary of some of Red Rocks' best multi-pitch climbs listed by difficulty.

Mescalito South, Cat in the Hat (5.6, 6 pitches)
With great and consistent climbing, big belay ledges, and an easy rappel down the route, Cat in the Hat is the friendliest and most popular route of its grade in Red Rocks.

Jackrabbit Buttress, Geronimo (5.6, 4 pitches)
This is a fun climb for those experienced at the grade with steep face and crack climbing with an exposed finish, but with some delicate holds.

Solar Slab Wall, Solar Slab (5.6, 11 pitches)
One of the best long routes of the grade anywhere with many variations.

Rose Tower, Olive Oil (5.7, 6 pitches)
Great varied climbing in a long crack to face to dihedral system with midday sun.

Angel Food Wall, Tunnel Vision (5.7, 6 pitches)
Fun chimneys with a cool tunnel-through pitch—a great climb with a short approach.

Angel Food Wall, Group Therapy (5.7, 6 pitches)
A wild big roof pitch at the top with some runout climbing lower, Group Therapy is a

good route for those comfortable with a bit of loose rock.

Mescalito North, Dark Shadows (5.8, 4 pitches)
It's hard to believe that the steep, dark, and ominous dihedral of Dark Shadows is rated only 5.8. The route is located in a tight canyon with large trees and pools of water—an atmosphere unique in Red Rocks.

Whiskey Peak, Frogland (5.8, 6 pitches)
Long, sustained, and deservedly popular, Frogland is one of the best of the moderate climbs in an area renowned for awesome moderates.

Cloud Tower, Crimson Chrysalis (5.8, 9 pitches)
This fantastic route is sustained at 5.8. There are many bolts when the climbing gets wide, which allows you to venture onto the face.

Burlap Buttress, Arrow Place (5.9, 3-5 pitches)
A great sunny route, opposite the popular Whiskey Peak Wall.

Solar Slab Wall, Beulah's Book (5.9, 3 pitches)
Fun climbing with a great new arête variation, often used as an approach to the upper Solar Slab.

Global Peak, Chuckwalla (5.9, 6 pitches)
A long remote approach guards this great face and crack climb in the rarely visited Mud Spring Canyon.

Black Velvet Wall, Epinephrine (5.9, 15 pitches)
One of the longest and best routes in Red Rocks, and certainly one of the best 5.9 routes in the world. Although rated "5.9," the chimneys on Epinephrine are slick, continuous, serious, and not to be underestimated.

Black Velvet Wall, Sour Mash (5.10a, 7 pitches)
With varied climbing, tons of thin cracks, tightly bolted face climbing cruxes, and an intriguing traversing roof to crack, Sour Mash is endless fun.

Black Orpheus Buttress, Black Orpheus (5.10a, 11 pitches)
Black Orpheus ascends a break in a huge overhung headwall via a cleanly fractured dihedral and has some of the best moderate crack climbing at Red Rocks.

Solar Slab Wall, Horndogger Select to Sundog (5.10a, 10 pitches)
Fun climbing on more delicate rock, this newer climb is sunny and perfect for more experienced sandstone climbers.

Black Velvet Wall, Dream of Wild Turkeys (5.10a, 11 pitches)
Long and sustained, Dream of Wild Turkeys tackles discontinuous features for over 1,000 feet of amazing climbing with nearly every pitch 5.9 or 5.10a.

Black Velvet Wall, Yellow Brick Road (5.10b, 10 pitches)
Yellow Brick Road is a two-pitch direct variation to Dream of Wild Turkeys. It is slightly harder, more sustained, and avoids the hardest slab cruxes of Dream of Wild Turkeys.

Black Velvet Wall, Prince of Darkness (5.10c, 6 pitches)
Amazingly sustained perfect edges up pitch after pitch of sport-bolted face, Prince of Darkness is one of the most classic face climbs in the U.S.

Eagle Wall, Eagle Dance (IV 5.10c A0, 10 pitches)
Long, sustained, and beautiful, nearly every pitch on Eagle Dance is 5.10 with a variety of climbing from thin crack to sustained edging face.

Eagle Wall, Ringtail (5.10d, 5 pitches)
Fun crack and dihedral climbing with a tightly bolted, thin edging crux.

Eagle Wall, Levitation 29 (5.11c, 10 pitches)
The classic 5.11 multi-pitch of Red Rocks, with an enduro crux freed onsight by Lynn Hill. It has everything from steep crack to roofs to endurance overhung thin face.

Whiskey Peak, Only the Good Die Young (5.11c, 5 pitches)
Wildly steep yet tucked away out of sight, Only the Good Die Young is easily the most neglected classic of its grade in Red Rocks.

Red Rocks Climbing Beta

Red Rocks Climbing Skills

Endless seas of perfect incut edges are the hallmark of Red Rocks face climbs. Unlike Yosemite, most Red Rocks crack climbs are actually face climbed while using the crack for protection and the occasional jam. For those not used to sandstone, take some time on easier climbs to get used to the often fragile rock, and above all else, do not climb on the rock the day or two after a rainstorm (longer if heavy rain), since the rock is significantly weaker when damp.

Climbing Gear

Red Rocks sandstone has many tapered cracks and a double set of nuts is essential. When cams are used, they are mostly in the thin to hand size (we'll warn you when bigger gear is needed). Tri-cams are useful for protection in pockets, as are very narrow head cams such as the larger sized Aliens. For many of the longer routes, many draws and slings are needed—it is common to clip more than 10 bolts on a single pitch. Extra rap slings and rap rings are a good idea for many of the routes, especially for trees and blocks. Most bolted stations have fixed rings or chains which eliminate ugly webbing tangles.

Ropes

Red Rocks is infamous for stuck ropes. Those great incut edges often snag ropes (some people call Red Rocks faces "velcro rock"), and raps down gullies or crack systems often end up with epic rope problems. While the long routes which you rap may seem like an obvious case for using double or twin ropes, these skinny ropes seem to get stuck more often than thicker lines. Also, many parties are used to using skinny tag lines or thin static lines. This is not recommended in Red Rocks due to the frequency that you have to re-lead up to retrieve ropes. If you have only a tag line or a static line, an easy lead up to retrieve your rope can be extremely dangerous. The most common solution is to have the leader trail another dynamic line, or have the follower backpack the second rope.

New and Delicate Climbs

he SuperTopo Red Rocks guide includes several lesser traveled or newer routes with more fragile holds than the more traveled classics. Use caution and pay extra attention to which holds are probably too thin to support a climber's weight for the following routes:

Geronimo
Horndogger Select and Sundog
Pine Nuts
When A Stranger Calls
This Ain't No Disco
Arrow Place
One-Armed Bandit
Aquarium

Non-Climbing Gear

A good supply of water is key, both for climbing days and for camping. Potable water is available at the campground, but it tastes bad. Fill up water containers from areas with better tasting water. Wear long pants and good approach shoes or boots to protect you from the often cactus-filled approach trails and the bushwacking descents. Use sunscreen and sun hats for warmer periods. Carry warm clothing and rain gear for anytime in the late fall through spring, where you can expect anything from hot periods to rain or snow.

About Anchors and the ASCA's Work

Until just a few years ago, most bolts on longer Red Rocks routes were terrible 20-year-old 1/4" bolts. Dan McQuade and friends spent a ton of time and energy replacing key anchors, and then in the last few years SuperTopo's own Greg Barnes, the Director of the American Safe Climbing Association, spearheaded rebolting efforts that have replaced almost 500 bolts on classic climbs in the canyons, including most routes covered in this Supertopo guide. All the work is done by volunteers— the ASCA has no paid staff. Please donate to the ASCA, a 501(c)(3) non-profit, as it doesn't yet receive enough support from the climbing community to keep up with all the bolts that need to be replaced. On average a new camouflaged 1/2" stainless bolt, hanger, drill bit, etc. for replacement in Red Rocks costs the ASCA about $9 in hardware costs alone. Visit www.safeclimbing.org for more information.

Environmental Ethics
Red Rocks is a desert ecosystem, and while the thorn and spine-barring plants may look (and feel) formidable, take care to reduce your impact. The number one way to do that is to stay on the main trails and avoid lesser traveled trails—even back-track if necessary. Bighorn sheep, peregrine falcons, and many other animals inhabit the canyons—respect them in their home.

Burros are feral (once domestic animals that have escaped to the wild) mule-like animals that were imported from North Africa to help miners in the 1800s. They are protected in Red Rocks, while in California they've been systematically removed from public lands for over 20 years. They are of most concern in Red Rocks while traveling on the highways at night, and speeding cars plus hard-to-spot burros have led to some serious accidents.

Unfortunately, the real environmental issues with Red Rocks are outside its boundaries and obvious to anyone who goes to Las Vegas more than once. The city is exploding in size and threatening to develop every scrap of land that it can get, somehow securing enough water for wasteful practices like artificial lakes in the middle of some of the suburbs. The hill across from the canyons, Blue Diamond Hill, has been the home of a gypsum mine for as long as anyone can remember. While the giant blasting (2 p.m. on Wednesdays usually) is annoying, the hill has blissfully blocked Vegas from view from most of Red Rocks. Unfortunately, this is likely to change, and unless enough pressure is put on the local government entities, high-end housing, golf courses, gated communities, and Wal-Marts may be only a few years away. Thankfully, development of this hill was delayed in May 2003 due to a big public outcry. See www.redrock.org for more info on how to help preserve Red Rocks.

Current Road and Weather Conditions
http://weather.yahoo.com/forecast/USNV0049_f.html or call the National Weather Service for local weather at 702-736-3854.

Getting There

Car Travel
Red Rocks is just west of Las Vegas and is accessed from various points in Vegas, and from Highway 160 from the Death Valley area. From almost any direction it's fastest to take the main Interstate highways into the city, although on weekends the heavy traffic flow from LA can long traffic jams across the desert from the west.

Despite what you'd expect from a map, if driving from the Bishop/Yosemite area it's actually much faster to take Highway 168 from Big Pine across Westgard Pass into Nevada, then down Highway 95. This takes about 4.5 hours. However, the views through Death Valley National Park, especially in late fall, winter, or early spring, are definitely worth seeing.

Sarah Felchlin

Air Travel

Las Vegas is one of the easiest, and cheapest, places to fly to in the world. However, huge conventions sometimes clog the airlines, drive prices through the roof, and fill up every hotel room. Plan ahead.

Loop Road

There is a $5 entrance fee to enter the loop. A Golden Eagle Pass (same as a National Park Pass but with a little golden sticker that costs $15) works to get you in free. If you already have a National Parks Pass, you can buy the Golden Eagle sticker here. Annual Red Rocks specific passes are also available for $20. Climbs accessed from the Loop Road have very limited parking hours. If you are staying after hours, and wish to avoid a $50 fine, call the late exit number (702-515-5050), where you must give detailed information on your car, the number of people, the route you're climbing, and emergency contacts. Late exit passes are only available for long routes in the canyons—not for sport climbing, bouldering, or hiking. Don't try to abuse the system. You WILL get fined for being in the Loop Road after closing with no pass. The pass only allows a few extra hours, and if you are still not out, you can get fined.

When to Climb

The longer routes at Red Rocks are in the canyons and many are usually too cold in the dead of winter. The best seasons are fall and spring, although south-facing routes are sometimes too hot (and therefore climbed even in mid-winter). Monitor current weather, as cold or hot spells can change your plans. Even in warmer spring and fall periods, cold storms happen regularly, and the sport, short trad, and bouldering areas of Calico Basin are often perfect when the canyons are stormy or drying out after a storm. Several local limestone areas are also perfect alternatives, and for truly desperate days, Powerhouse Rock Gym (next to Desert Rock Sports on West Charleston Boulevard) offers indoor overhung leads and hot showers.

June through August is usually so hot that no one dares climb except in the coldest canyons. Air temperatures well above 100 degrees are common. Local high-altitude limestone climbing is the best choice if you're in Vegas this time of year.

Staying in Red Rocks

Camping

Unfortunately, there is only one campground in the Red Rocks area—the BLM 13 Mile Campground. It is located on West Charleston (Route 159), one mile from Calico Basin Road. While the 13 Mile Campground is new and fairly large, it fills quickly in prime season. Both drive-in and walk-in sites are $10 (which is odd since you can have two cars at a drive-in site but only one at a walk-in). Currently there are about 40 sites, but plans are under way to double the size of the campground. Large groups should reserve some of the group sites, which are only $25 a night for up to eight cars and 20 people. These are often reserved 6 months in advance for peak times. Visitors Center: 702-363-1921.

If full, Vegas hotels or a long drive to the west to find a camping spot are the only options. If you can sleep in your car, the back lots of many large casinos are usually hassle free. Take note that cheap hotels are difficult to find and almost non-existent on weekend nights. It is illegal to camp at the trailhead for Black Velvet Canyon or anywhere in that area.

Recently Added Bolts

Many classic Red Rocks moderates have recently had some bolts added. Sometimes added by the first ascent party, and sometimes added by unknown parties, these bolts may be removed by other climbers wishing to preserve the difficulty and danger level of the climb. Some bolts indicated in the SuperTopo may or may not remain, and if they are missing, do not be overly surprised. Check the SuperTopo Route Beta section and the SuperTopo Climber's Forum for more current info at:

http://www.supertopo.com

Restaurants

There are endless restaurant options all over Las Vegas. The main concentration of eateries near Red Rocks are along Charleston Boulevard and Sahara Avenue, and Rainbow Boulevard, which runs perpendicular to the two. Every fast food chain and tons of restaurants and casino buffets dot the city.

Groceries

Several brand-new large grocery stores are on Charleston Boulevard near Red Rocks. By the time you read this there will be even more so take your pick. There is a Starbucks inside every one, and there is a Starbucks outside in the strip mall in front of every one as well. We're not joking.

At the intersection of Highways 159 and 160 near Blue Diamond (on the way out to Black Velvet Canyon from the campground) is a new gas station with a small selection of food and supplies.

Water

Carry plenty of water—especially on the south-facing routes. Dehydration is no fun and impairs judgement. Get water at the campground, the visitors center, or nearby stores. The water at 13 Mile is particularly nasty, so stock up ahead of time if you can.

Library/Internet Access

West Charleston Library (6301 West Charleston Boulevard; 702-878-3682) is the easiest to find and has about 20 internet terminals. You have to have a library card to use the terminals, but they are easy to obtain.

Sahara West Library (9600 West Sahara Avenue; 702-507-3630) is the quickest to get to and has around 50 Internet terminals that you can use for free for an hour, but amazingly they are all filled much of the time. You currently do NOT need a library card, just a photo ID such as your driver's license. It also has a discarded book salesroom out front where you can pick up great reading material at a quarter per paperback and 50 cents per hardback. Just down the street is a large mall/movie theater complex.

Climbing Gear

Desert Rock Sports (8201 West Charleston Boulevard; 702-254-1143, www.desertrocksports.com), on Charleston Boulevard as you drive into town, is a full-service climbing shop with a huge gear selection and knowledgeable staff. One of the folks you'll likely see there is one of the owners, Mike Ward, who's been doing long FAs in Red Rocks since the 1970s (including several of the routes in this book). Powerhouse Gym, located in the same building, is a good option for rainy days and also offers affordable showers.

Climbing Guides

American Alpine Institute: 360-671-1505; www.mtnguide.com
Jackson Hole Mountain Guides: 702-254-0885 ; www.jhmg.com
Mountain Skills: 505-776-2222; www.climbingschoolusa.com
National Outdoor Leadership School (NOLS): 307-332-4784; www.nols.edu
Sky's The Limit: 800-733-7597; www.skysthelimit.com

Other Guidebooks

Rock Climbing Red Rocks by Todd Swain offers a full guide to sport climbing and information on many climbing routes in the canyons.

The Red Rocks of Southern Nevada by Joanne Urioste was recently reprinted, and has detailed written information on many canyon routes not covered by any other guide.

Islands in the Sky by Dan McQuade, Randy Leavitt, and Mick Ryan is a guide to limestone climbing all over Nevada, most of which is concentrated close to (and sometimes even in) Red Rocks. www.rockfax.com

Las Vegas Limestone by Roxanna Brock covers all Las Vegas area limestone climbing. www.VegasClimbing.com

Red Rocks Bouldering by Rob Jenson, and *Las Vegas Bouldering Guide* by Jared McMillen, cover local bouldering. Also by McMillen is the *Red Rocks Sport Climbing Guide*.

Crime

Las Vegas is a big city with big city crime. Never leave your wallet in your car, conceal valuables, and be especially careful at canyon trailheads. If possible, conceal any evidence that your car belongs to a climber. Thieves specifically target climbers' cars because they know they will be gone all day. A common trick is to break into a car, find a wallet, remove a single credit card, then carefully lock the car back up. By the time you figure out that a card is missing, thousands of dollars have been charged at local casinos. Also, it is not uncommon for valuables like mountain bikes to be simply ripped off of locked racks on the car, sometimes leaving parts of the fork behind.

Camping near the city to the west along Highway 160, which is a heavily traveled road to the satellite town of Pahrump, runs the risk of violent crime and should be carefully considered. Gun shells litter the campsites, and most sites near the road are illegal to camp at.

Animals and Sharp Plants

Be very careful around the abundant cacti and sharp desert vegetation—a glance will tell you that the plants in Red Rocks know how to defend themselves. It's a good idea to carry a pair of tweezers for cactus spines.

Rattlesnakes, scorpions, tarantulas, and wasps are present but rarely seen.

Peregrine falcons nest in the canyons—do not disturb them if you see them (besides, they are bold and have a history of attacking climbers).

Please give Desert Bighorn sheep a wide berth in the unlikely event that you see them up close (half a mile away up a 5th class wall is more common).

Rest Days

The human zoo of Las Vegas, especially The Strip, must be viewed at night. The roller coasters, pirate shows, fountains, and endless extravagantly decorated casinos are reminiscent of the orgies of the Roman Empire in its heyday. There are so many bright lights in Vegas—especially the one out of the top of the Luxor's black pyramid—that Las Vegas is the most intensely bright spot on earth as seen from space.

For other "rest" day activities, there are many excellent hikes in Red Rocks, notably Bridge Mountain and Turtle Mountain. Full information on these is available at the BLM visitors center. Fun hikes up the various canyons can also be good times to scope the approaches to routes without the weight of your gear. Those with mountain bikes can explore the big new array of trails out near the entrance to Black Velvet Canyon. There are also longer excellent single tracks south of Highway 160, all on hard-packed and often rocky terrain. A quality mountain biking map is available at the mountain bike store right next to Desert Rock Sports/Powerhouse Gym. Tire kits (and tweezers) are essential as these trails wind in and out of sharp plants.

The desert tortoise among spring wildflowers.

Greg Barnes

SuperTopo Mission

- Help climbers ascend and descend routes quickly, efficiently, and safely by creating the most accurate and informative climbing topos ever published.

- Capture the mystery, adventure, and humor of climbing by publishing the histories, anecdotes, and outrageous stories of each route.

- Promote clean climbing by publishing the most up-to-date rack info as well as hammerless ratings for each pitch.

- Stress the importance of low impact climbing and promote stewardship of the environment.

Visit www.SuperTopo.com Before Each Climb

There is much more beta available for free on the SuperTopo web site: www.supertopo.com. Visit the web site before your climb to be sure you have the latest information.

The web site offers additional free beta for each climb:

- photo galleries
- trip reports
- route condition updates
- closures and rockfall warnings
- route beta email alerts

The web site is packed with general Red Rocks info:

- free downloadable color topos
- road and weather conditions
- everything you need to know about staying in Red Rocks
- good routes for first-time Red Rocks climbers
- general trip planning info

Protect Red Rock Canyon

by Jed Botsford, Climbing Ranger

Sarah Felchlin

Why do you climb at Red Rock Canyon? Is it one of your favorite places to climb when it is cold everywhere else? Do you like it because of the variety of the climbing, the wilderness experience while climbing tall routes in the canyons, the sport routes with quick approaches, or the large amount of bouldering? It seems as though every climber has a different reason for why they climb at Red Rocks. One theme that climbers can all agree on is that the climbing access at Red Rock Canyon is worth protecting.

Protecting the Desert Environment

What can you do to protect the fragile desert environment while climbing at Red Rock Canyon National Conservation Area? Remember and practice some of the Leave No Trace principles.

Plan Ahead and Prepare

A nice hot cup of coffee is great to get you going in the morning, but it also gets other things moving. Plan to go to the bathroom before you leave the parking lot instead of waiting until you are at the base of the crag. Human waste does not decompose in the desert soils and toilet paper is trash.

When you are climbing a tall route, always carry a headlamp and warm clothes. All too often climbing parties head up a route which takes much longer than was expected and get caught in the dark.

If you are not sure if you will be able to do the approach, climb the routes and get back to your car before the closure of the Scenic Drive, call for a Late Exit Permit and save yourself a $50 ticket. The permit is free and easy to get by calling 702-515-5050.

Travel on Durable Surfaces

While you are hiking, stay on established trails to avoid trampling cryptobotic soils. Red Rock Canyon has been a popular climbing area for a long time. There is always an established trail leading to a climb or crag. Take a few minutes to find the trail instead of cutting across open desert or straight up to the climb.

Sandstone is a porous rock and absorbs water during a rainstorm. Allow the rock to dry out for at least 24 hours after a rain. There are some great limestone crags around Red Rocks and Las Vegas that can be climbed on when the sandstone is wet.

Pack It In, Pack It Out

Pack out all your toilet paper, tape, cigarette butts and left-over food. How many times have you arrived at the base of a tall route and right where the climb starts there is an orange peel or some other type of trash? The orange peel may biodegrade but it can take up to a year in the desert for it to disappear.

Respect wildlife

Seeing a wild horse or burro is a great experience, but remember that wild horses and burros are federally-protected animals and it is illegal to harass or feed them.

Climbing Access

"What can I do to help protect the climbing access at Red Rock Canyon?" This question is one of the most common questions I am asked while I am on patrol. My reply depends on the situation, but here are some great ways to protect climbing access at Red Rock Canyon.

Get involved with your local climbing groups, such as the Las Vegas Climbers Liaison Council and join the Access Fund. Participate during project days when land managers and climbing groups are working together on a trash pick up at a local crag, or a chalk cleaning session.

Talk with the land managers before you decide to put up a route. Find out if there are any bolting restrictions. Red Rock Canyon has two wilderness areas: Rainbow Mountain and La Madre Mountain Wildernesses. As of the summer of 2003, the BLM does not allow any new bolting to take place in the Wilderness areas of Red Rocks.

The BLM will be writing a Wilderness and Climbing Management Plan in the near future. By getting involved and talking with the BLM, your comments can be incorporated into both the Wilderness and Climbing Plans that will affect climbing directly.

One of the most popular bouldering areas in Red Rocks is the Kraft Boulders. The access into Kraft is through private property. As long as climbers approach the bouldering area by parking in the BLM designated parking areas, walking on the dirt roads to the boulders and not cutting across private property, the Kraft Boulders will be open for a long time to come.

If you would like to learn more about Leave No Trace ethics check out their website at: http://www.lnt.org.

If you would like to contact either of the climbing rangers at Red Rocks, feel free to call 702-515-5138 or 702-515-5042.

Larry DeAngelo

If you are lucky, you may run into Bighorn sheep. These were spotted below the Brownstone Wall.

Free Climbing Ratings

USA Yosemite Decimal System	UIAA	France	UK	Australia
5.1	I	1	M	4
5.2	II	2	D	6
5.3	III	2+	3A/3B VD	8
5.4	III+ / IV	3-	3B/3C HVD	
5.5	IV+	3		10
5.6	V-	3+	3C/4A S · 4A/4B HS	12
5.7	V	4	4A/4C VS	14
5.8	V+	4+		16
5.9	VI-	5	4C/5B HVS	
5.10a	VI	5+		18
5.10b	VI+	6A	5A/5C E1	19
5.10c	VII-	6A+	5B/6A E2	20
5.10d	VII	6B	5C/6A E3	21
5.11a	VII+	6B+		
5.11b	VIII-	6C		22
5.11c		6C+	6A/6B E4	23
5.11d	VIII	7A		24
5.12a	VIII+	7A+	6A/6C E5	
5.12b	IX-	7B		25
5.12c	IX	7B+		26
5.12d		7C	6B/6C E6	27
5.13a	IX+	7C+		28
5.13b	X-	8A	6C/7A E7	29
5.13c	X	8A+		30
5.13d		8B	6C/7A E8	31
5.14a	X+	8B+		32
5.14b	XI-	8C	7A/7B E9	33
5.14c	XI	8C+		34
5.14d	XI+	9A	7A/7B E10	35
5.15a		9A+		36

Cam Sizes by Brand

Ref Size*	BD Camalots	CCH Aliens	Metolius Cams	Trango Big Bros	Wild Country Friends
0.4"	.1 red	.33 black	00 gray		
0.5"	.2 yellow	.375 blue	0 purple		0 red
0.6"	.3 purple	.5 green	1 blue		.5 orange
0.75"	.4 gray	.75 yellow	2 yellow		1 yellow
1"	.5 pink	1 red	3 orange		1.25 brown
1.25"	.75 green	1.5 orange	4 red		1.5 sky
1.5"	1 red	2 purple	5 black		2 pink
1.75"	1 red	2.5 gray	6 green		2.5 royal
2"	2 yellow	2.5 gray	7 blue		3 navy
2.5"	2 yellow		8 purple		3.5 purple
3"	3 blue		9 burgundy		4 black
3.5"	3.5 gray		10 dark blue		4 black
3.5-4.5"	4 purple			1 red	5 silver
4.5-5.5"	4.5 red			2	
5.5-7"	5 green			3 green	6 plum
7-8"				3 green	
8-12"				4 blue	

*"Ref size" is the optimal crack width for a given camming unit. It is not the range given by the manufacturer.

Understanding the Maps

Topo Symbols

Right-facing corner		Roof	⊥⊥⊥⊥	Bolt	x
Left-facing corner		Ledge	⊤⊤⊤⊤	Rappel anchor	
		Slab	/////		
Straight-in crack		Belay station	❶	Face climbing	
Groove		Pitch length	130' ●	Pine tree	
Arête				Oak-like tree	
Flake		Optional belay	○	Bush	
				Knob	○
Chimney		False belay	⊘	Hole	●

Notes on Rack

• "nuts" refers to any nut, stopper, or chock. "micro"= #1, 2; "sml"= #3-5; "med"= #6-8; "lrg"= #9-13
• for cams, "2 ea .75-1.5" means bring two sets of all sizes between .75" and 1.5". Check the cam size chart to see which cam corresponds to which crack size.

Notes on Topo

• "belay takes .6-1" means, while leading the pitch, save enough .6-1" cams and nuts to build a natural anchor.
• a number next to a tree is its height.

Topo abbreviations

ow = offwidth
lb = lieback
p = fixed piton
R = runout (dangerous fall)

Metric system conversions

1 inch = 2.54 centimeters
1 foot = 0.305 meters
100 feet = 30.5 meters
50 yards = 45.7 meters

Overview graphics

Canyon Wall	
2WD/4WD dirt road	··················
Road or State Route	——⑩——
Federal Highway	——⑩——
Hikers' trail	—·—·—·—·—
Climbers' trail	—————————
Cross-country travel	·················

Star Ratings

★★★★★ - undisputed classic
★★★★ - excellent climb
★★★ - good climb
★★ - okay climb
★ - barely included in this book

Red Rocks Overview Map

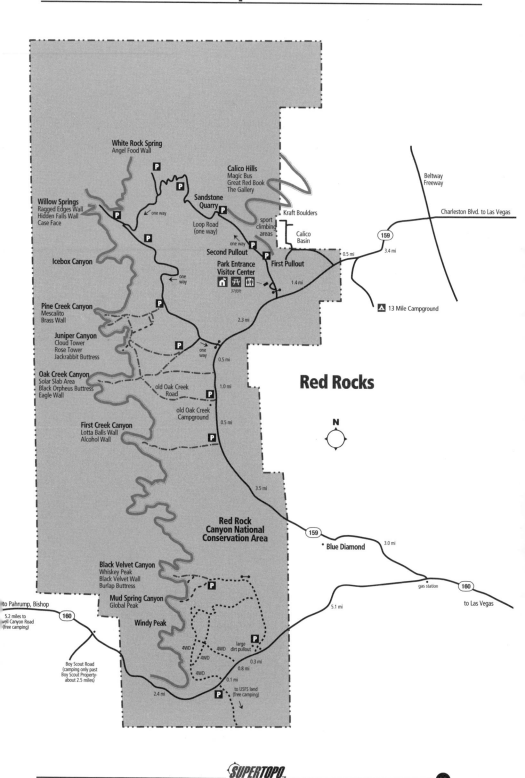

White Rock Spring
Angel Food Wall

Calico Hills
Magic Bus
Great Red Book
The Gallery

Beltway Freeway

Willow Springs
Ragged Edges Wall
Hidden Falls Wall
Case Face

Sandstone Quarry

Kraft Boulders

sport climbing areas

Calico Basin

Charleston Blvd. to Las Vegas

Loop Road (one way)

one way

one way

Second Pullout

First Pullout

Icebox Canyon

Park Entrance Visitor Center
3700ft

0.5 mi

3.4 mi

159

1.4 mi

▲ 13 Mile Campground

Pine Creek Canyon
Mescalito
Brass Wall

2.3 mi

Juniper Canyon
Cloud Tower
Rose Tower
Jackrabbit Buttress

one way

0.5 mi

Red Rocks

Oak Creek Canyon
Solar Slab Area
Black Orpheus Buttress
Eagle Wall

old Oak Creek Road

1.0 mi

old Oak Creek Campground

0.5 mi

N

First Creek Canyon
Lotta Balls Wall
Alcohol Wall

3.5 mi

Red Rock Canyon National Conservation Area

159

Blue Diamond

3.0 mi

Black Velvet Canyon
Whiskey Peak
Black Velvet Wall
Burlap Buttress

gas station

160

Mud Spring Canyon
Global Peak

5.1 mi

to Las Vegas

to Pahrump, Bishop

160

5.2 miles to
...ell Canyon Road
(free camping)

Windy Peak

4WD

4WD

large dirt pullout

4WD

0.3 mi

0.8 mi

Boy Scout Road
(camping only past
Boy Scout Property-
about 2.5 miles)

4WD

0.1 mi

2.4 mi

to USFS land
(free camping)

Windy Canyon

Despite its size and relatively easy access, Windy Canyon is rarely visited. The southernmost major formation of Red Rocks, Windy Peak has a huge south-facing wall with a long approach, and a smaller east-facing wall with a much shorter approach. A complicated network of roads confuses many trying to approach this canyon, yet it is fairly simple to navigate them by leaving from the road out to Black Velvet Canyon. With a remote and isolated feeling, Windy Canyon is both literally and figuratively about as far as you can get from the busy sport climbing crags.

Greg Barnes

A Blockade Runner
B Jackass Flats
C Diet Delight

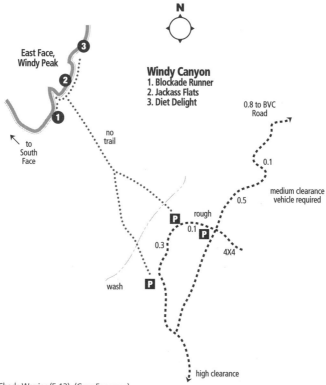

East Face, Windy Peak

Windy Canyon
1. **Blockade Runner**
2. **Jackass Flats**
3. **Diet Delight**

0.8 to BVC Road

← to South Face

no trail

0.1

medium clearance vehicle required

0.5

rough

P   0.1   P

0.3

4X4

wash   P

high clearance

Dan McQuade, Chode Warrior (5.13). (Greg Epperson)

Windy Peak, East Face

Greg Barnes

Windy Peak is the southernmost major rock formation on the main Red Rocks escarpment. The 400-foot east face has dark rock with a prominent roof on its left, and is easily seen from the parking area. Despite the relatively short distance, the lack of a good trail plus a bit of bushwacking make the approach a bit longer than you first expect, although it is still one of the shorter approaches at Red Rocks.

Approach

Diet Delight
From the parking area, hike down into the main wash and up to the East Face. There are no real trails, just various burro trails. The best path ascends a bit left of center of the East Face, heading up below Jackass Flats. Once near the base, small steep cliffs are below Jackass Flats. Traverse right under the cliffs and over to the large brown face until under Diet Delight. Skirt the bushes on the right, looking around a bit to help avoid extra bushwacking. Diet Delight starts up a small pillar to the thin crack in the middle of the largest clean face, which is bounded on the right by a pillar.

Jackass Flats
Scramble up a bushy 3rd class ramp just left of the start of Diet Delight, then traverse down and along a large blocky ledge to the base of the chimney. Beware of cacti on the ledge.

Blockade Runner
On the left side of the small brown buttress at the bottom of the Diet Delight descent gully is a clean dihedral. Approach as for the other routes, but traverse left past the big gully once at the base of the cliff.

Descent

Diet Delight
From the top of Diet Delight, you can either scramble down and rap from a large tree into the gully (nasty cactus problems, two ropes needed, not recommended), or scramble up 50 yards, then scramble around and into the gully. Beware of cactus both at the topout for the climb and all along the descent. The gully is 3rd/4th class (optional rappel at one point) once you reach it, but take care to find the easiest way of getting there. From the base of the gully, either scramble back over to your packs, or descend straight to the car if you have your gear with you. Note that the excellent one-pitch 5.8 Blockade Runner is just to the right at the base of the gully.

Blockade Runner
From the top of the climb, traverse behind the big boulder and rap from slings 100 feet into the bottom of the Diet Delight descent gully. From here, return to your packs and scramble back to the car. It's easiest to descend the ridge that you came up.

Jackass Flats
From the top of the second pitch, traverse left and rappel once with a 60m rope into the bottom of the Diet Delight descent gully. Reverse the approach to the car.

Diet Delight 5.9★★★

Time to climb route:	**2-3 hours**
Approach time:	**30-45 minutes**
Descent time:	**1-1.5 hours**
Sun exposure:	**sunrise to midday**
Height of route:	**400'**

Diet Delight is not your standard Red Rocks edge pull. It has smooth rock and fractured climbing up cracks and dihedrals. Crack technique, liebacking and stemming are all required, and several sections have challenging protection.

FA: George Urioste and Joanne Urioste, 2/77.

Strategy

The first pitch is a thin crack with smooth rock for the feet at the crux, and is a bit runout.

Right off the belay on the second pitch is a somewhat tricky section of flakes with poor protection. Luckily, just as it gets really steep and right before the crux, there is a piton and a bolt. The steep, reachy section right above the bolt is the crux. Only a few moves gains a big ledge.

Near the top of the route, some routefinding is needed as the route winds its way through short lieback cracks, large blocky dihedrals, and a cool finishing arête just left of an overhung crack/dihedral. Take extra care just after topping out to avoid the many cacti waiting to fill your rope with little needles.

Both Jackass Flats and Blockade Runner are fun climbs which are easily done in combination with Diet Delight, and both require only a single 60m rope to rappel. If doing Jackass Flats, you will pass right by

the base of Diet Delight to approach, while Blockade Runner is on the opposite side of the descent gully.

Retreat

Retreat off trees and bolts on a newer route to the right. Near the top of the climb, you must leave gear.

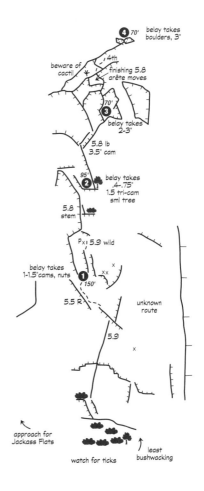

Diet Delight	Pitch			
	1	2	3	4
Free difficulty				
≥5.10				
5.9	●	●		
5.8			●	●
5.7				
5.6				
≤5.5				

Rack

nuts: 1 set
cams: 2 ea .5-3"
        1 ea 3.5"
optional: extra .75" cams

Jackass Flats 5.6★★

Time to climb route: **1-1.5 hours**

Approach time: **30-45 minutes**

Descent time: **30-45 minutes**

Sun exposure: **sunrise to noon**

Height of route: **300'**

Jackass Flats is a great end of the day route. It is a fun two-pitch jaunt up okay rock with a quick descent by rappelling into the bottom of the Diet Delight descent gully. A long hand crack in mediocre rock on the second pitch is the highlight of the climb.

FA: Joe Herbst and Matt McMackin, 2/73.

History

In the early 1970s Joe Herbst was exploring the southern crags of Red Rock Canyon. Even then, before the visitors center and paved loop road, it provided a more serene wilderness experience than the more heavily used northern part of the area. On the prominent cliff of the east-facing slopes of Windy Peak is a varnished jutting roof that resembles a chess knight. Joe was joined by Matt McMackin for a climb on the flat face below this roof. Matt was a high school student and a friend of Randy Grandstaff. As they lead up to the left side of the large roof on the last pitch, they managed to get their rope stuck. Joe now says, "We felt like real jackasses!" The flatness of the face, the equestrian theme of the "chess piece," and the rope misery combined to produce the route name.

– Larry DeAngelo

Strategy

There are rarely crowds on Jackass Flats. There is a bit of chimney climbing and loose rock, and some bushwacking on the approach, but most of the climbing is fun with good protection. The descent, a 95-foot rappel from slings around a constriction, is quick and easy.

Retreat

You must leave gear to retreat. Note that fixed slings are often present at the 5.5 stem halfway up the second pitch.

A. Blockade Runner   5.8★★★★

FA: Unknown

With crack and face climbing on great rock, Blockade Runner is a fun addition to climbing other routes in the area. The crux of Blockade Runner is climbing around large hollow blocks (not really loose, but disastrous if they came off, so you climb around). Be careful, as you could dislodge a block with excessive force. Carry a 60m rope to rappel, and it's a rope stretcher, so be careful. The descent is around the corner to the right into the same descent gully as Diet Delight and Jackass Flats.

Jackass Flats		1	2
Free difficulty	≥5.10		
	5.9		
	5.8		
	5.7		
	5.6	●	
	≤5.5		●

Jackass Flats 5.6★★

nuts: 1 set
cams: 2 ea .6-3"

A. Blockade Runner 5.8★★★★

nuts: 1 set
cams: 1 ea .6-.75", 3"
       2 ea 1-2"

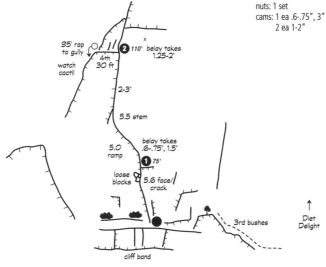

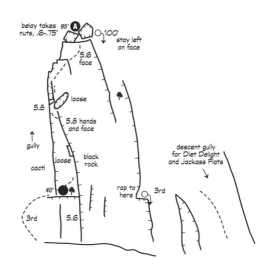

Mud Spring Canyon

Rarely visited, with no developed trails and very long approaches, Mud Spring Canyon is one of the most spectacular of the canyons at Red Rocks. A complex approach, bushwacking, cactus and shrub oak, beautiful pools nestled in a sculpted stone canyon—all add up to an experience unlike most anywhere else in Red Rocks. With the long approach times and shady exposure of the climbs, plus the nice swimming holes, this is a great choice for longer, warmer days.

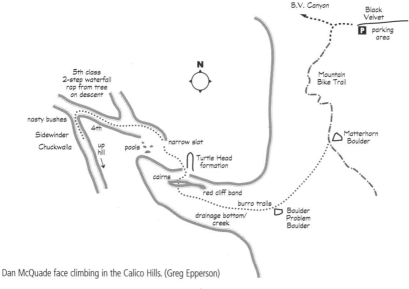

Dan McQuade face climbing in the Calico Hills. (Greg Epperson)

Global Peak

Global Peak—about 2 hours into the approach.

Greg Barnes

Tucked away deep in Mud Spring Canyon, Global Peak is not an obvious formation until you get near it. It's an impressive sight—rounded up top like a Tuolumne dome, with a nearly featureless 800-foot northeast face. By the time you get a good view of it, you will be excited to do some climbing instead of all the bushwacking and scrambling. The rock is featured steep face climbing with lichen patches here and there, and generally appears somewhat uninviting due to the lichen. Stellar climbing awaits though, and the hike, while long and tedious, keeps the crowds away.

Approach

The approach is long with a lot of bushwacking and routefinding. It takes most people at least 3 hours. Park at the Black Velvet Canyon (BVC) parking lot. Hike up the old road/mountain bike trail toward BVC for a few hundred yards, but when the BVC trail takes off right, follow the winding bike trail left for about 0.5 mile to a large triangular boulder ("Matterhorn Boulder"). From here, the bike trail heads south, but hike southwest toward the mouth of Mud Spring Canyon and a huge brown boulder (don't get too high, stay in the easy flats). From the giant brown boulder, head up into the canyon following burro trails to the right of the canyon bottom—again, don't go too high, but follow the main burro trail. Hike up the canyon for about a half mile—you will get closer to a red rock band on the right (Chinle formation, like the junky stuff below Frogland). Near the end of the rock band is the first place it looks possible to cut up—go up here, following a few large old cairns. There is a small roof on the top of a 300-foot

brown rock formation above this point ("the Turtle Head"); it's easy to spot even in the dark on the way down since the roof cuts against the neon-lit skyline. Cut right above the red rock band for a bit to get to a large ramp which heads up and left at the base of the Turtle Head formation. There are some boulder problem/bushwacking approach difficulties here. Follow the ramp up and around the corner to a spectacular view of the North branch of Mud Spring Canyon, and your first fairly good view of Global Peak. Contour down and right on a ledge system, passing through a short "narrows" slot, to the canyon bottom above some killer swimming pools. From here, a long section up the main canyon bottom gets you to a bushy ramp to the left. In this canyon you encounter boulder-hopping, bushwacking, and a few 5th class sections (see next paragraph), the last of which has a rap anchor off a tree. Follow this bushy ramp up a few hundred yards past some tricky spots to the base of the sheer wall. Chuckwalla heads up the blank face to the left of the obvious corner system (Sidewinder), and starts above a low-angle ramp, going up a 30-foot-tall flake, then left and back right past three bolts to an anchor at a break in angle on the face.

The first "5th class section" in the canyon bottom is easy with only a 20-foot chimney/corner that is probably more like 4th class—it's easy to hand up packs. The second (with the rap anchor) is a two-step waterfall/giant boulder blockage, about 40 feet high. At the first step you face climb 15 feet up on the left wall about 30 feet before the overhung boulder, then step onto a ledge and walk to the start of the second tier. The face is difficult with a pack, but without, there's a nice finger lock that is not too scary; you can haul packs once you're up. The second tier is a surprisingly slippery chimney up the right side of the big boulder—a good spotter is all you really need—then haul the packs up with a rope, and fix the line to the rap anchor for your partner(s) to grab (or you could set up a belay).

Descent

Rappel and reverse the approach. The raps will take 30-45 minutes, and the descent is not much faster than the approach. Remember to leave your harnesses on and keep a rope on top of your pack for the rappel past the 40-foot 5th class section.

Turtle Head

Greg Barnes

The crux routefinding of the Chuckwalla.

Chuckwalla 5.9★★★★★

Time to climb route: 4-6 hours

Approach time: 3 hours

Descent time: 3-4 hours

Sun exposure: never (fall/winter) all day (summer), partial (spring)

Height of route: 800'

Chuckwalla is guarded by a long approach yet is an awesome face route in the middle of beautiful and unique surroundings. The climbing is continuous, stiff, and runout by Red Rocks standards; it can be compared to well-protected face climbs in Tuolumne. Chuckwalla is intimidating, striking a nearly perfect straight line up a monolithic blank wall. With its newly replaced bolts and a rack requiring little pro other than nuts, it's a stellar backcountry adventure.

FA: George Urioste, Joe Herbst, and Joanne Urioste, 6/78.

History

This route was originally called Chuckawalla 21 because there were 21 bolts and "chuckawalla" was the phonetic pronunciation of a local lizard. Two bolts have been added, and the spelling corrected, hence the name, Chuckwalla.

George and Joanne Urioste initially spotted the formation while descending from the Velvet Wall, one canyon north. Joanne gave it the name Global Peak because, "Well, it was round." Impressed with the route potential, they worked their way back into the canyon in May 1978. They climbed the nearby route, Sidewinder, which was, of course, named after another desert creature. But the Uriostes were mainly attracted to the line of Chuckwalla,

even though it would require bolt protection on some blank face climbing sections. They made plans to return and work on the new route.

Meanwhile, Joe Herbst also had his eye on the formation, which he intended to name "The Spirit Kiln." He picked out a line and was planning to scout it, but had not yet gotten around to checking it out. The area was so remote that he felt no rush. In fact, he felt mild pride at simply having spotted the route potential in this inaccessible canyon. He was taken by surprise when the Uriostes invited him to come along on the Chuckwalla first ascent.

Although Joe's initial reaction was a disappointed, "Doggone!" he was impressed with the Uriostes' line, which he considered better than his own idea. Beyond that, it brought him to the realization that George and Joanne had the ability and willingness to put up excellent new routes.

The route went well. Even though Joe viewed bolts with skepticism, he could not help but be impressed that George placed all 21, drilling by hand, in one day.

On the descent, they passed a small tower, the top of which was composed of several precariously stacked blocks. Observing the potential danger to future parties, Joe suggested that they kick down the loose top layer. Unfortunately, this was a suggestion he made AFTER rappelling past it. He believed he was safely off to the side when George dislodged the threatening debris. A large block took a freak bounce and came straight toward him. "It was really close," he said. "It was like playing dodgeball, except you could die. I was pretty shaken up."

– Larry DeAngelo

Chuckwalla	Pitch	1	2	3	4	5	6
Free difficulty	≥5.10						
	5.9	●	●				
	5.8			●	●		
	5.7						
	5.6						
	≤5.5					●	●

Strategy

Start very early, especially on shorter days. Most people can expect to start and end the day with headlamps. With its northern exposure and the great swimming holes half way up the approach, this could be a fun warm weather climb if you get an early enough start to avoid the worst of the desert heat.

The first pitch is the psychological crux for most. It has substantial runouts and tricky pro. The second pitch has a runout off the belay, and a section of slopey holds which come as a surprise after relying on good edges, but it is the continuous nature of this long pitch which forms the crux.

The fourth pitch is continuous, and protection in the crack sometimes spotty, so it's wise to stop for good placements whenever possible. This is a long pitch, and it's easy to run out of draws for clipping nuts. Use long slings to avoid rope drag.

The fifth pitch is "only 5.5" but very run out on loose holds.

Obviously a route with a 3 hour approach is a poor choice for bad weather; no bivi permits are available for this canyon.

Retreat

Rappel with two ropes from any pitch, and retrace the approach.

George Urioste follows the first pitch, 2002

Greg Barnes

Rack

nuts: 2 ea sml, med
       1 ea lrg
cams: 1 ea .4-.5"
       2 ea .6-1"
       1 ea 1.25-2"
many slings and quickdraws

120' **6**

5.6
var.   5.4

150' **5** x x

5.5 R
loose

5.4 R

1.25" on
right

160' **4** x x

5.8 fingers

5.6 R
x x **3** 130'

5.6 lb
hands

5.8

x x **2** 155'

old unnamed
Urioste route

10
bolts   5.9

old
slings

150' **1** x x

nut | 5.9

.75"
cam, nut

5.7 R
sling
edge/plate

Sidewinder

Black Velvet Canyon

Black Velvet Canyon has the highest concentration of quality longer routes at Red Rocks. Unfortunately, they are nearly always in the shade, and while they are perfect in spring and fall, once temperatures drop, the canyon is rarely visited. Black Velvet Canyon is accessed from dirt roads off of Highway 160, the road from Las Vegas to Pahrump (and Death Valley). Recent development of mountain biking trails in this area means you should be careful on the drive in, since bikers sometimes end up on the road (it also means that you should bring your mountain bikes—the trails are great!). It is ILLEGAL to camp at the end of the road at Black Velvet, and rangers will fine you if you are caught. However, since the road is not gated, you can get VERY early starts—especially important for those doing Epinephrine.

Greg Barnes

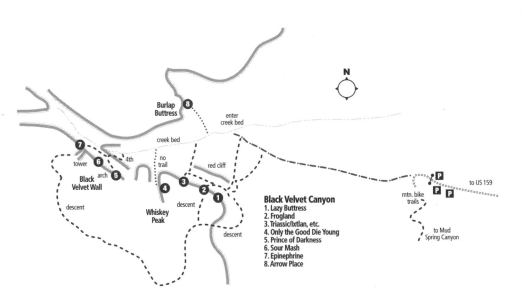

Black Velvet Canyon
1. Lazy Buttress
2. Frogland
3. Triassic/Ixtlan, etc.
4. Only the Good Die Young
5. Prince of Darkness
6. Sour Mash
7. Epinephrine
8. Arrow Place

Whiskey Peak

Overshadowed by the main Black Velvet Wall, but closer to the road, Whiskey Peak Wall is packed full of amazing climbs, and many headed to Black Velvet Wall change their plans once they look up at the splitter cracks on their left. The right side of the wall has a collection of steep cracks, and hidden far around right is an overhung wall, which is home to one of the steepest 5.11s in Red Rocks. The left side of the wall—the one first encountered and closest to the road—has some of the best moderate climbing in Red Rocks.

Approach

Accessed by an independent dirt road far from the gated loop road, Black Velvet Canyon is an easy and convenient area to approach. The obvious trail heads up from the parking area toward the mouth of the canyon. After a gentle climb, the trail splits—one branch dives down into the creek bed and continues up the canyon and to Black Velvet Wall and the other goes steeply up left to Frogland.

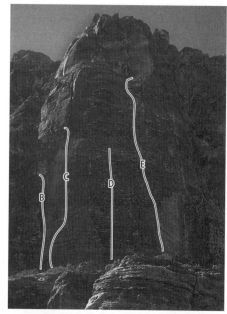

Greg Barnes

B	Mazatlan	D	Sand Felipe
C	Ixtlan	E	Triassic Sands

Frogland
The trail bypasses a small cliff band to the left, then contours right through brush to the base of the route, which starts at a 30-foot-tall white flake at the base of a big, brown left-facing corner. The approach takes about 30 minutes.

Only the Good Die Young
Between the main part of Whiskey Peak and the 4th class cliff band at the base of Black Velvet Wall are a couple of large gullies. The first of these, which heads up along the edge of Whiskey Peak, is the approach for Only the Good Die Young. As this route sees little traffic, some bushwacking is needed. You can also traverse right from the bottom of Wholesome Fullback on 3rd class ledges and brush to access the gully. Keep your eye out for the first bolt as the overhung wall above the gully is so steep that many walk right by the start of the route, not expecting it to begin where it does.

Whiskey Peak Crag
See page 46 for detailed approach information.

Frogland

Greg Barnes

Descent

Frogland

The descent for Frogland is simple and requires no rappels, yet the gully is loose and has a few short 3rd class downclimbs. Luckily, huge cairns guide you down the correct parts of the gully, and even if you make a mistake, it is easy to backtrack. Once back at the level of the base, a well-worn trail works back to Frogland. You can cut down early if you didn't leave anything at the base, but the best trail by far is the approach trail, so look out for it. The descent takes about an hour, depending on how fast you travel down rocky gullies.

Only the Good Die Young

Descend down to the right on 4th class ledges to a 60-foot rappel off a tree, or up to a long 3rd class ledge to gain the gully. Drop back down the gully to the base (lots of bushwacking and 3rd class), or if you have all your gear, you can go up through the notch and down the Frogland descent. There are no real trails due to the lack of traffic in the gully.

Greg Barnes

Frogland 5.8★★★★★

Time to climb route: **3-4 hours**

Approach time: **30 minutes**

Descent time: **1 hour**

Sun exposure: **sunrise to mid-morning**

Height of route: **700'**

Long, sustained, and deservedly popular, Frogland is one of the best of the moderate climbs in an area renowned for awesome moderates. The varied climbing, routefinding, and slightly runout slab crux make Frogland a definite challenge for the 5.8 leader. As with other Red Rocks classics, the biggest obstacle is usually the crowds. Luckily, there are some great nearby routes that have long been overlooked. Schaeffer's Delight—an old, long-forgotten Urioste route, which has just been rebolted—is one of the best 5.7 face climbs around.

FA: George and Joanne Urioste, 5/78.

History

In May of 1978, the spring at the mouth of Black Velvet Canyon was the source of a persistent pond. The pond itself was home to a noisy contingent of frogs. Back in the Gunks, which was the area that George and Joanne came from, there was an entire set of climbs with "land" names: Birdland, Roseland, Disneyland. Joanne connected the Gunks naming convention to the local croakers, and the route became Frogland.

Though the Uriostes were no strangers to hammer work in general, and bolting in particular, a minor landmark was passed on Frogland's third pitch. Leading to the left and crossing the main dihedral, Joanne stepped onto a small ledge and drilled the first bolt of her life. In the light of the prodigious quantities of protection bolts they were about to place in the next few years, one might wonder if the moment held any special meaning. "No serious significance," said Joanne. "Only the lactic acid in my forearm."

– Larry DeAngelo

Strategy

Frogland gets early morning sun and early morning crowds, but in colder weather the sun soon departs the wall and the climb is frigidly cold. Quicker parties who are up at daybreak can have the route to themselves when most people think the canyons are too cold. In prime weather, starting late in the day can also work. Two ropes allow retreat from the first two pitches on bolts, but after that gear would be required to retreat, although some trees can be used.

The first pitch crux is slick face and/or liebacking, but only a few moves gain a bolt and easier climbing. The fourth pitch has a tricky section, where the most obvious line—heading up to a roof then left—is the hardest variation, and heading left earlier drops the difficulty by quite a bit. The fifth pitch slab crux is the psychological crux for most, and even after the bolt-protected slab, a stemming/finger dihedral up to a looming giant chockstone intimidates many. Luckily, a hand crack offers protection for the tunnel under the left side of the chockstone.

Retreat

Retreat with two ropes from the bolted anchors and/or trees on the first two pitches. Some trees to the right of the route, and several constrictions/large blocks/flakes, offer various potential retreat points on Pitches 3 and 4, although gear may need to be left. Also, the probability of rope snags is very high on the third and fourth pitches. Gear would likely need to be left to retreat from high on the route.

Frogland	Pitch	1	2	3	4	5	6
Free difficulty	≥5.10						
	5.9						
	5.8	●		●	●	●	
	5.7		●				●
	5.6						
	≤5.5						

A. Unknown   5.5★★★

Huge jugs and spectacular climbing bypass
an intimidating roof on the excellent first
pitch. Rappel directly down Schaeffer's
Delight, which is a great toprope or lead.

B. Schaeffer's Delight   5.7★★★★

FA: Mike Petrilak, Mike Ward, George Urioste, 9/84.

This is one of the best face climbs at Red
Rocks. While the route is 5.7, a runout and
slightly loose start combined with fragile
holds high on the pitch, make Shaeffer's
Delight a somewhat serious lead. Anyone
unsure of their abilities should climb the
first pitch of the Unknown route to its
left and toprope Shaeffer's Delight before
leading it.

History
When first climbed in 1984 this was a
single-pitch face route. George's friend,
Mike Petrilak, was an avid climber and
mountaineer whose mobility had been
reduced by a broken hip suffered in the
Tetons. George placed the protection bolts,
then retreated so that his friend would have
the pleasure of the first lead. Mike named
the route after Schaeffer's Beer, his favorite
beverage.

– Larry DeAngelo

C. Lazy Buttress   5.6 R★★

FA: Matt McMackin, Nanouk Borche, Joe and Betsy Herbst, 10/73.

Awkward stemming with poor protection,
plus several hollow sections, make Lazy
Buttress a challenge. While "only" 5.6,
the cruxes are all wide stemming or
chimneying, and thus care should be
taken for those unfamiliar with chimney
climbing. Rappel Schaeffer's Delight with
two ropes. The route actually continues
higher, but is low quality with loose and
contrived climbing.

History
In the early 1970s, Nanouk Borche arrived
in Las Vegas from her home in France. Her
boyfriend Serge Gousseault had recently
died in a two-week epic while attempting
a winter ascent of a new route on the
Grandes Jorasses in the company of René

A	Unknown	**C**	Lazy Buttress
B	Schaeffer's Delight	**D**	Unknown

Desmaison. In the aftermath of the tragedy,
the media attention and reminders drove
Nanouk to the United States.

Joe Herbst met Nanouk on a
backpacking trip in the Grand Canyon.
The trip had been organized by one of the
original Red Rock outdoorsmen, Howard
Booth. Unfamiliar with the area, Nanouk
asked Howard if she should wear her heavy
boots for the trip. Howard reasoned that
for a winter backpack, good boots were
appropriate. He didn't realize that she came
from a serious Alpine milieu and her "heavy
boots" were the extremely rigid ice climbing
footwear of the era. Within a few miles, she
developed a bad case of blisters. She solved
the problem by completing the hike (to the
bottom of the canyon and back) barefoot.

– Larry DeAngelo

D. Unknown   5.8★★★

A great two-pitch climb up a dihedral with
good pro, this is a perfect addition to a day
of climbing in the area. With two short
pitches, only a single 50m rope is needed,
and the second pitch is good practice for
many routes in Red Rocks which have tight
dihedral sections.

Rack

Frogland 5.8★★★★★
nuts: 1 ea sml, med, lrg
cams: 2 ea .6-3"
many slings

A. Unknown 5.5★★★
nuts: 1 set
cams: 1 ea .6-4", 2 ea 2-3"
two ropes

B. Schaeffer's Delight 5.7★★★★
cams: .6-1.25"
7 quickdraws
two ropes

C. Lazy Buttress 5.6 R★★
nuts: 1 set
cams: 2 ea .6-1.25", 1 ea 1.5-3"
two ropes

D. Unknown 5.8★★★
nuts: 1 set
cams: 1 ea .6-.75", 1.5-3", 2 ea 1-1.25"

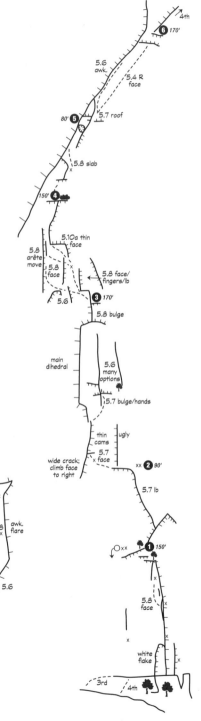

Peter Kohl on the fabulous 8th Wave, Calico Basin. (Greg Epperson)

Whiskey Peak

Approach time: **30 minutes**

Sun exposure: **early morning**

Height of routes: **40′ to 320′**

The middle section of Whiskey Peak is home to some of Red Rocks' best splitter cracks and some excellent face climbs. While bordered by Frogland and the huge routes of Black Velvet Wall, and with original long finishes up the towering wall above, most rappel these climbs after one to three pitches.

Approach

Accessed by an independent dirt road far from the gated Loop Road, Black Velvet Canyon is an easy and convenient area to approach. The obvious trail heads up from the parking area toward the mouth of the canyon. After a gentle climb, the trail splits—one branch dives down into the creek bed and the other climbs steeply up left to Frogland. The trail bypasses a small cliff band to the left, then contours right through brush to the base of Frogland, which is easy to spot by a 30-foot-tall white flake at the base of a big, brown left-facing corner. The Whiskey Peak crag routes begin 100 yards to the right.

Descent

Descend all routes by rappelling. Follow the same trail back to the car.

A. The Misunderstanding   5.9★★★

FA: Dave Anderson, Randal Grandstaff, 1975.

Steep and clean in a beautiful, brown dihedral, this route is an obvious line. However, it is also quite obvious from the ground that it is a WIDE crack. The second pitch crux—an endurance wide crack—is done mostly with liebacking, and relatively little true offwidth technique is used. Yet some offwidth skills—especially foot bridging—are needed, and placing protection while lieback/stemming in a steep slick dihedral scares many away.

History

Dave Anderson's name appears here and there in the Red Rocks guidebooks and is usually associated with a clean, high-quality route. A committed mountaineer from Seattle, Dave loved climbing and built his life around it.

Joe Herbst mentions that Dave Anderson was a "strong, really fine climber; very adventurous." Mark Moore, with whom Dave shared many climbing adventures, recalls Dave's mastery: "We were high on the Salathé Wall and he was leading the roof out to the headwall. I was dehydrated and feeling pretty spaced out. The rope was dangling way out there, swaying and twisting. But for Dave, it was just business as usual."

Dave was skiing in Utah when he was caught in an avalanche and broke his leg. When the rescue helicopter came to transport him to the hospital, it crashed and Dave was tragically killed. The loss is even greater, Mark says, because Dave's commitment and love of the mountains "could have made him the Fred Beckey of his generation."

– Larry DeAngelo

B. Mazatlan   5.10d R★★★★

FA: Dave Anderson, Randal Grandstaff, 1978.

Mazatlan is as good as it looks—long, beautiful, clean crack climbing in a dihedral. Unfortunately, the crux is right off the deck and protected only with RPs, which are difficult to place from technical stems. For most people, this first section is dangerous, and a good collection of tiny nuts and Screamers are essential. The rappel anchor is bomber bolts and chains.

C. Ixtlan   5.11c★★★★

FA: George and Joanne Urioste, Dan Goodwin, 1981.

The third pitch offwidth crack to roof of Ixtlan is one of the most distinctive features of Black Velvet Canyon. Rarely done, it is actually quite reasonable, and there is no doubt that the first pitch thin face is the technical crux. However, the third pitch offwidth is burly and requires that hallmark skill of the offwidth climber—brutal grunting and suffering. Often overlooked, the second pitch is excellent climbing requiring both jamming and liebacking skills on somewhat hollow rock.

History

Carlos Castaneda's books have been many things to many people. They burst into popularity during the drug-oriented hippie culture of the late 1960s when his initial "Teachings of Don Juan" outlined a path to Knowledge. This was a path that happened to be paved with mind-altering hallucinogens. The book was a milestone of speculative anthropology, and ushered in a series of follow-up books that redefined reality, cast aside conventional perceptions, and expanded spiritual horizons. They also provided a good source of route names such as "Tales of Power" and "Separate Reality." His third book was "Journey to Ixtlan," which he probably never anticipated would inspire the name of the consciousness-expanding offwidth crack in Black Velvet Canyon.

One fan of the Castaneda books was Dan Goodwin, better known by the nickname Spider Dan for his exploits climbing skyscrapers. Immediately before the ascent of Ixtlan, Spider Dan spent Memorial Day climbing Chicago's Sears Tower. He climbed the John Hancock Center a short time later, and the World Trade Center (South Tower) in 1983. His November, 1998 ascent of the World Trade Center (North Tower) was the last before its destruction in 2001.

Ixtlan's line is beautiful and compelling, but is defended by a stretch of blank sandstone at the base. The necessity of a few bolts was never an obstacle to George Urioste. The first pitch involved ordinary thin face climbing. A little help from a hook, and the bolt was placed. The clean offwidth on Pitch 3 required a more creative approach.

Although it has been reported elsewhere that George Urioste fabricated some oversized wooden cams for the offwidth pitch, the story is a little different. George says, "Well, I did make the wooden cams, but that was for a different route. On Ixtlan we didn't use them. On the first ascent, I

led the first two pitches to the base of the offwidth. Dan led on Pitch 3, trying to protect it with large Titons and tube chocks. All the gear got in the way so you couldn't free climb the crack. I went back with a scissors jack from a car. I put it in the crack and cranked it until it stuck, then leaned over and drilled the protection bolts." If a problem can be solved with an ingenious mechanical contrivance, it is an absolute certainty that George will find the solution!

–Larry DeAngelo

D. Sand Felipe   5.10a★★

FA: Unknown.

A fun, well-bolted face climbing pitch, Sand Felipe is a good way to round out the day, and also easy to toprope when descending from Triassic Sands.

E. Triassic Sands   5.10c★★★★

FA: Joe Herbst, Larry Hamilton, 1972.

Deservedly one of the most popular 5.10 cracks in Red Rocks, Triassic Sands has an unforgettable roof crux, and a super-long hand/off-hand crack that would chew you up if it were not for the abundant face holds that bring the climbing down to the 5.9 range. The third pitch is long, excellent crack and face climbing, and the whole climb is one of the very best shorter multi-pitch climbs around.

History

Triassic Sands was the first "real" rock climb of significant length at Red Rocks. It was originally climbed as an aid route in 1972 by Joe Herbst and Larry Hamilton, as a warm-up for the Salathé Wall. One look at the wall and you can easily see that this route does not skirt the main challenges or wander through broken zones of weakness. Joe and Larry were two of the most productive early Red Rocks climbers, and together accounted for a number of serious routes including both the Rainbow Wall and the Aeolian Wall.

In the late 1970s enthusiastic young Randal Grandstaff turned his attention to free climbing Triassic Sands. As a teenager a few years earlier, Randal served an apprenticeship as ropemate of Joe Herbst. Building on that experience, and with a few Yosemite seasons under his swami belt, he was now starting to build a name of his own. Randal's plan was to climb the beautiful hand crack about 30 feet to the right of the aid line. This required some difficult climbing through an initial overhanging section. Randal showed up with a couple of aggressive young friends and went to work. They climbed the overhang and gained the hand crack above. By all rights, they should have been done. The rock becomes less steep, and plentiful face holds ease the difficulty.

Unfortunately, an obstacle barred their way. Just below the belay spot, a horribly loose flake blocked the crack. It was several feet wide, and was so delicately balanced that merely touching it caused it to shift. The climbing looked suicidal, so they called it a day and went down. Randal was never one to pass up a good story, so he told Joe Herbst of their effort and the high quality of the climbing.

The challenge intrigued Joe. During a visit from his good friend and trusted partner Tom Kaufman, they went up to have a look. Tom anchored himself in a hanging belay just below the death flake, giving himself enough slack to pendulum to the side. Joe led up to the flake. Using handholds to the side, he positioned himself to get a foot onto the precarious block. The next move would require the ultimate in mutual confidence. Joe gave the signal. Tom swung to the right. Joe cranked with all his might. The huge flake toppled to the left and cartwheeled down the face, exploding dramatically on the slopes below. With the threat thus removed, they completed the free ascent uneventfully.

– *Larry DeAngelo*

F. Wholesome Fullback   5.10a★★★★★
FA: Cal Folsom, Lars Holbek, 1975.

Often overlooked, Wholesome Fullback is probably the best single pitch of 5.10a crack climbing in Red Rocks. The first pitch is awesome: thin finger crack right off the deck, splitter hand crack, a tricky face traverse under a small roof, a technical lieback/finger crack crux, and then seemingly endless perfect hand jams to a ledge 160 feet off the deck. Many people are scared off by the chimney of the short second pitch, but it is trivial climbing, and to top it all off, you can toprope the splitter 5.10d crack top pitch of Our Father on the way down.

History
This is the same Lars Holbek who is famous in whitewater circles and who assures me that his frequently misspelled name should truly be "Holbek." During one of his Red Rocks trips, Lars climbed with Mark Moore. They planned to hop a freight train and ride back to the Pacific Northwest. While still in Las Vegas, a guard was inspecting the cars and spotted Mark. Lars kept his head down and didn't move. Somehow he was never spotted and only Mark was thrown off the train.

But the story has a twist. Mark stuck out his thumb to hitchhike and immediately got a ride. He beat the train to Mojave, where he was able to get back on and complete the trip. Ironically, Lars got off in Las Vegas to look for his friend, so the two climbers did not meet up again for several months.

– *Larry DeAngelo*

G. Our Father   5.10d★★★
FA: Rick Wheeler, Joe Herbst, Randal Grandstaff, Vern Clevenger, 1977.

Our Father is rarely led because of the serious runout on 5.9 slab and large loose blocks on the second pitch. The third pitch 5.10d dihedral crack is the highlight. Easily toproped on the rappel from Wholesome Fullback, this pitch is a must-do.

History
What a strong first ascent team! Joe Herbst recalls, "It was just one of those great days. The weather was perfect and our confidence was high. When Vern was along, you felt sure you could climb anything! The route name? Someone else must have thought it up—I don't even remember where it came from."

– *Larry DeAngelo*

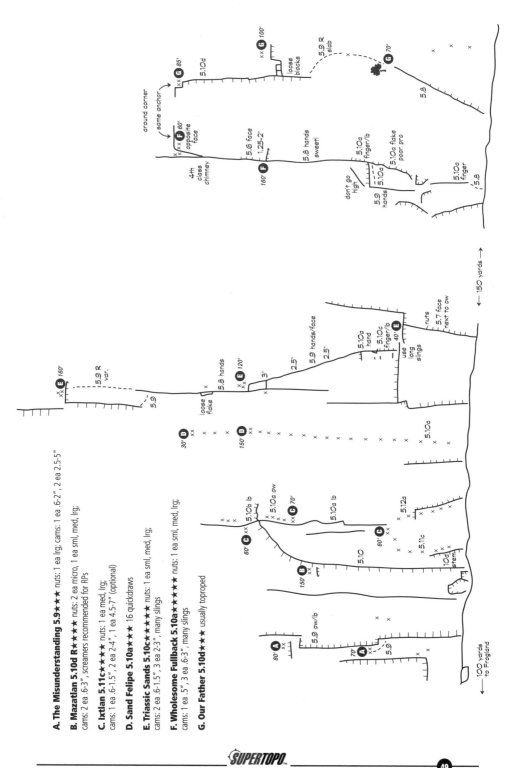

A. The Misunderstanding 5.9★★★ nuts: 1 ea lrg; cams: 1 ea .6-2", 2 ea 2.5-5"

B. Mazatlan 5.10d R★★★★ nuts: 2 ea micro, 1 ea sml, med, lrg; cams: 2 ea .6-3", screamers recommended for RPs

C. Ixtlan 5.11c★★★★ nuts: 1 ea med, lrg; cams: 1 ea .6-1.5", 2 ea 2-4", 1 ea 4.5-7" (optional)

D. Sand Felipe 5.10a★★★ 16 quickdraws

E. Triassic Sands 5.10c★★★★★ nuts: 1 ea sml, med, lrg; cams: 2 ea .6-1.5", 3 ea 2-3", many slings

F. Wholesome Fullback 5.10a★★★★★ nuts: 1 ea sml, med, lrg; cams: 1 ea .5", 3 ea .6-3", many slings

G. Our Father 5.10d★★★ usually toproped

Only the Good Die Young

5.11c★★★★

Time to climb route: **2-3 hours**

Approach time: **35 minutes**

Descent time: **1 hour**

Sun exposure: **never**

Height of route: **350'**

Wildly steep yet tucked away out of sight, Only the Good Die Young is easily the most neglected classic of its grade in Red Rocks. Quick to access and fairly short, and just across the way from the super popular Black Velvet Wall, many strong parties will easily combine Only the Good Die Young with other routes in a day. Since the cruxes are tightly bolted, those at their limit can easily work through the difficulties. The ASCA replaced the bolts in October 2001.

Strategy

While the climb is five pitches, all are short, and as it is overhung right off the deck, warming up on the classic crack climbs around to the left is recommended. With the high grade other parties are a rarity.

The 5.11 sections are all bolt ladders. However, the 5.10d crux right off the deck is pretty tricky so be careful. To reduce rope drag on the fourth pitch, consider reaching back and unclipping the first bolt on the traverse, and also just skipping the last bolt on the traverse under the roof (it is an original Urioste bolt—the only original protection bolt that was 3/8").

Retreat

It is possible to retreat from any of the first three pitches with a single rope if you are careful to stay to the right. However, as the climb is overhung, if you come off the ramp you might not be able to get back on. Two ropes are far safer for retreating. Use care rappelling into the steep loose gully at the base, as rocks are easy to dislodge onto your partner.

Only the Good	Pitch				
	1	2	3	4	5
Free difficulty					
5.11	•		•		
5.10	•		•		
5.9					
5.8					
5.7					•
≤5.6					

Rack

nuts: 1 ea sml, med, lrg
cams: 2 ea .6-1.5"
        1 ea 2-3"

Peter Croft cranks on Desert Gold (5.13). (Greg Epperson)

Black Velvet Wall

Huge and sheer, the full scale of Black Velvet Wall isn't apparent until you stand at the base. Packed with tons of Red Rocks' highest quality and longest moderate routes, Black Velvet Wall is the centerpiece of the easily accessed Black Velvet Canyon, and in the opinion of many climbers, the centerpiece of Red Rocks itself. Although the routes stretch to 12 pitches or more, none ascend the full 2,500 feet of the wall—even Epinephrine cuts out right on an escape ledge near the top. Most of the climbs are six to eight pitches and located on the "small," clean black face at the lower left of the wall. Steep, long, and sustained, Black Velvet Wall routes offer some of the best climbing in the world.

Approach

Black Velvet Canyon is at the southern end of the escarpment and thus the approach road is not off the gated Loop Road, so you can start in the middle of the night if desired. The approach trail is straightforward until almost at Black Velvet Wall and takes about 45 minutes. Just before the wall, climb a 100-foot 4th class cliff to the left of the wash bottom. It

Greg Barnes

A	Prince of Darkness	**E**	Overhanging Hangover
B	Dream of Wild Turkeys	**F**	Sour Mash
C	Yellow Brick Road	**G**	Epinephrine
D	The Gobbler		

is steep and some may want a toprope from an experienced leader.

The routes along the main wall all start from a huge brushy slope/ledge system. Prince of Darkness, Dream of Wild Turkeys, Yellow Brick Road and The Gobbler start about 60 feet left from the bottom left of the huge arch. Sour Mash climbs up to the right end of the gigantic roof. For Epinephrine, from the top of the 4th class, walk down back into the canyon bottom, then about 100 yards up the wash to a point below the right side of the huge tower (Black Tower). Look for bolts up the gray wall straight below the ominous chimney above. The left line of bolts is 5.8, and the bolts have all been replaced by the ASCA. The right line has bad bolts and crumbly rock. While this first 50 feet of 5.8 is fun, linking it to the next part of the pitch creates a lot of rope drag, and many parties skip it by ascending the unprotected 5.4 ramp to the right.

Larry DeAngelo

Descent

From the base of Black Velvet Wall, retrace the approach trail. Some may wish to rappel the 4th class, or to have a more experienced climber downclimb the 4th class several times to ferry less experienced climber(s) pack(s) down the wall.

Dream of Wild Turkeys Rappel

Yellow Brick Road and The Gobbler are variations of Dream of Wild Turkeys and use the same rappel. Almost everyone rappels from these climbs, and while SuperTopo includes upper pitches not included in other guides, we have not done the walk-off from the top. If you choose to walk off, be competent and prepared.

There are many rappel stations on the various routes, and your choice of rap route largely depends on climbers below. Since there are so many choices, we do not attempt to give all the possible rap lengths. Use knots or other backups to avoid rappelling off the end of your ropes!

Overhanging Hangover Rappel

Rappel with two 60m ropes from the anchor. You will have to do a second rappel off a small tree on the first pitch ledge of Sour Mash, unless you are willing to do some 5th class downclimbing.

Sour Mash Rappel

Rappel the upper pitches until you end up on the raps down Fiddler on the Roof (see

The Epinephrine descent follows this ridge down then drops off left.

topo). Pitches 2-4 of Sour Mash involve large traverses and are difficult to rappel. While there is no fixed anchor at the top of Pitch 1, there are trees which could be slung for retreat. To rappel from Pitch 2, use a draw or two for directionals to regain the start of the pitch.

Epinephrine Descent

With good light and proper routefinding, the descent from Epinephrine takes about an hour or two. However, it has been the site of epic descents lasting overnight or longer. The key to the descent is to scope it from the parking lot. The common mistake is to attempt to cut down too soon, which can lead to an epic multi-pitch rappel down a huge and loose chimney system. From the pine tree, hike southeast to a notch, then contour up and south to the main ridgeline. Follow huge cairns down the top of the ridge for almost half a mile—resist the urge to head down sooner. Several small cliff bands must be avoided or downclimbed along the way. Eventually a pile of large cairns—4 or 5 all in one spot—mark the start of the descent down steep dirt and rocks. After about 200 yards, the cairns lead back left for about 100 yards, then down through a slabby part of a cliff band to the notch above Frogland. From here it is easy going down the well-marked Frogland descent gully. It is also possible to go back to the base of Black Velvet Wall, but it is an ugly bushwacking experience and not recommended.

The Epinephrine descent.

Prince of Darkness

5.10c★★★★★

Time to climb route:	**3-4 hours**
Approach time:	**45 minutes**
Descent time:	**1-1.5 hours**
Sun exposure:	**midday on upper part of route**
Height of route:	**1200'**

Amazingly sustained perfect edges up pitch after pitch of sport-bolted face, Prince of Darkness is one of the most classic face climbs in the U.S. With nearly no moves easier than 5.8 or harder than 5.10a, and with no rest ledges, it is heaven for 5.10 climbers, as long as you bring a butt bag or a comfortable harness for the hanging belays. You need a few nut and thin cam placements, but with up to 15 bolts per pitch, the rack mainly consists of quickdraws.

History

George and Joanne Urioste, Mike Ward, and Bill Bradley climbed this route in July 1985. The noteworthy aspect of the enterprise was that Joanne was already a few months pregnant and was feeling the debilitating effects of morning sickness. Her challenges were compounded by a summer heat wave reaching 117 degrees.

The route name was chosen by Bill Bradley as an ironic twist on the local bolting controversies. Dissension had blossomed around the Uriostes' bolting of Dream of Wild Turkeys. Following this, several members of the "adventure" contingent put up Rock Warrior (Richard Harrison, Jay Smith, Nick Nordblom) as their idea of what a Velvet Wall route should be. Unpersuaded, the Uriostes continued with the heavily bolted Yellow Brick Road

and Prince of Darkness, which had even more bolts. The "Prince of Darkness" name referred to the satanic level of evil such bolting was supposed to represent. Naturally, the response was Sandstone Samurai (Paul Van Betten, Nick Nordblom), which had even less.

Amazingly, George was generally unaffected by the rustles of controversy. He had a vision of what a route should be, and he was willing to work quite hard to realize that vision. One of his primary guiding principles was the creation of a route that was elegant and "couth." He looked for clean direct lines, secure and comfortable belays, safe levels of protection, and a lack of loose rock or vegetation. By George's reckoning, Prince of Darkness succeeded on all these points. The only weakness that he noted was a lack of variety—move after move of steep thin face climbing with no change of pace.

As it happened, this was the last of the big face-climbing routes that the Uriostes did for a while (see notes of impending parenthood in first paragraph). And it was the last they did bolting by hand and hammer, the old-fashioned way.

– *Larry DeAngelo*

Strategy

Prince of Darkness is basically a six-pitch sport climb and has the crowds to prove it—get there early. It's always a good idea to bring additional gear to climb surrounding routes in case a slow party is ahead of you.

The 5.10b slab crux on the second pitch (first bolted pitch) is the crux of the climb for many people. The final pitch 5.10c crux involves thin lieback/crack moves past bolts. The moves into the crack on the crux pitch can be very difficult for shorter people.

Retreat

You can rap with two ropes from any pitch, and it is possible to rap to the left and down the classic runout route Rock Warriors at some spots (NEVER do this if anyone is on that route!). It's also possible to rap to the right and down Yellow Brick Road, Dream of Wild Turkeys, and/or The Gobbler.

		Pitch					
Prince of Darkness		1	2	3	4	5	6
Free difficulty	≥5.10		●	●		●	●
	5.9				●		
	5.8						
	5.7						
	5.6	●					
	≤5.5						

Dream of Wild Turkeys

5.10a★★★★★

Time to climb route: **3-5 hours**	
Approach time: **45 minutes**	
Descent time: **1.5-2 hours**	
Sun exposure: **morning to afternoon high on route**	
Height of route: **1200'**	

Dream of Wild Turkeys tackles discontinuous features for over 1,000 feet of amazing climbing with nearly every pitch 5.9 or 5.10a. The first route up the main Black Velvet Wall, Dream of Wild Turkeys is the classic mostly face route of the grade in Red Rocks. Most of the surrounding routes covered in the SuperTopo guide are variations on this route.

History

The first ascent of Dream of Wild Turkeys was completed by George and Joanne Urioste in June 1980. This route tackled the central, smooth part of the Velvet Wall. Their original expectation was that there would be a significant amount of direct aid, so they set off on the climb with haulbags, planning for a big-wall type of effort. Serendipity intervened. The wall was not really smooth. The numerous little flakes and nubbins quickly destroyed their haulbags, but also provided the means for free climbing.

They realized that free climbing the face between natural features would require a major bolting effort. This climb therefore became the next step in the "route construction" philosophy they had originated with the ascent of Epinephrine, and refined on Eagle Dance. Though these routes are widely climbed and enjoyed today, they were the source of local controversy at the time of the first ascent.

The prevailing ethic at the time valued an ascent starting from ground to summit in one push, with great efforts taken to avoid placement of bolts or pitons that scar the rock. The strength of many climbers' conviction is evident from the fact that on some occasions they literally risked their lives to avoid placing a bolt, and frequently backed off or declined lines that could not be climbed with natural (and clean) protection. Such climbers were outraged that the Uriostes would fix ropes and heavily bolt their way up "blank" faces. (It should be noted that by current standards, the Uriostes were very conservative, placing all bolts on lead, by hand and hammer, and usually finishing their routes on summits.)

With that as background we must turn to North Wales, where Ed Drummond and Dave Pearce climbed A Dream of White Horses in 1968. Royal Robbins wrote an article about it in the 1975 book Hard Rock. He opened, "A Dream of White Horses— one of the great names, fulfilling Geoffrey Dutton's dictum that a name should tell you something about the climb or the way it was done. One glance at Leo Dickinson's masterful photograph explains it: that great sheet of spray leaping from the sea, rearing from excited waters like a splendid white stallion, and two figures fastened to the rock just out of reach of the tormented foam..." Because the Uriostes were approaching their routes in a manner that was out of step with the contemporary values, they were generally shunned and disrespected by much of the growing Las Vegas climbing community. And that's what the name says about how the route was done: though ostracized and made to feel like "turkeys" they persisted with their dream and put up one of the classic lines at Red Rock.

– Larry DeAngelo

		Pitch									
Dream of Wild Turkeys		1	2	3	4	5	6	7	8	9	10
Free difficulty	≥5.10			●		●		●				
	5.9		●				●	●		●	●	
	5.8											
	5.7											
	5.6	●										
	≤5.5							●				

Strategy

Start early because the route shares a first pitch with the even more popular Prince of Darkness. Quick parties can bypass slower parties by climbing The Gobbler, or if there are slow parties three to four pitches up, by climbing Yellow Brick Road. Prince of Darkness, Overhanging Hangover, and Sour Mash are all options as well, and since all these climbs require at most the rack you need for Dream of Wild Turkeys, you will already be prepared.

Thin, technical face climbing on incut edges is the hallmark of Red Rocks, and almost every crux on the Black Velvet Wall involves this sort of climbing. However, the slabby crux sections often stymie climbers, especially the 5.10a at the top of the crack on the fourth pitch. Most people rap after the seventh pitch (where Prince of Darkness ends), but the ninth pitch, a 5.9 bolted dihedral, is one of the finest on the route and should not be missed.

Retreat

Rappel from anywhere on the route, and due to the surrounding climbs, many options are available. Two ropes are required, and longer ropes give you more flexibility. Beware of the fourth pitch—it is much better to rappel down Yellow Brick Road, as the crack eats ropes with a vengeance. Likewise, if you rap down to The Gobbler, it is far better (and more fun!) to rap off the roof than down the chimney/crack system.

Yellow Brick Road

5.10b★★★★★

Time to climb route:	**3-5 hours**
Approach time:	**45 minutes**
Descent time:	**1.5-2 hours**
Sun exposure:	**morning to afternoon high on route**
Height of route:	**1200'**

Yellow Brick Road is a two-pitch direct variation to Dream of Wild Turkeys. It is slightly harder, more sustained, it avoids the hardest slabby cruxes, and thus is an excellent variation for those climbing at the grade.

History

By the time the Uriostes, with Mike Ward and Bill Bradley, began this route in the spring of 1985, they were experienced in leading long, bolt-protected first ascents. One challenge was simply having the hardware to adequately protect the routes. Doubts were already beginning to surface about the security of the 1/4" bolts that climbers had been relying on for anchors. Mike had a bad experience at about this time on Zodiac in Yosemite. The first move of that route was a hook leading to a 1/4" aid bolt. As soon as he weighted the bolt, it snapped, dropping him twenty feet to the ground. They continued and finished the route, but the experience was educational.

In order to retain some level of safety on their Red Rocks routes, they attempted to place a sufficient number of bolts to preserve a reasonable redundancy of anchors. This required many bolts and hangers. To satisfy their hardware needs, a small production line was set up in George's garage. The hangers were cut from pieces of angle iron originally intended for bed frames. They were cut, drilled (two different hole sizes), deburred, carabiner hole beveled, and painted. Many a Friday night was spent in the little factory, creating the supplies for the weekend's pitches.

One unusual item they fabricated for this route was the "trail sign" plaque marking the fork where Yellow Brick Road deviates from Dream of Wild Turkeys. Joanne writes, "The sign was done with mischievous intent (i.e. bolts were "bad," so a sign must be "badder"). I forget whose idea it was (maybe mine!)."

– Larry DeAngelo

Strategy

The crack climbing on the first pitch (after Dream of Wild Turkeys breaks straight right) is an outstanding finger crack, and it is a highly recommended variation. It also cuts one pitch off the overall climb (unless the link variation is used when climbing Dream of Wild Turkeys).

Retreat

It's possible to rappel from anywhere on the route with two 50m or 60m ropes.

Yellow Brick Road		Pitch 1	2
Free difficulty	≥5.10		
	5.9		●
	5.8		
	5.7		
	5.6	●	
	≤5.5		

The Gobbler 5.10a★★★★

Time to climb route:	**1 hour**
Approach time:	**45 minutes**
Descent time:	**1 hour**
Sun exposure:	**rare**
Height of route:	**330'**

Done the month following the first ascent of Dream of Wild Turkeys, The Gobbler is really a three-pitch independent starting variation to that classic route. Outstanding and technical, its first pitch is different from most of the rest of the routes on the wall with thin positive edges on a slick slab and little else to use (often just edges for your feet or hands). The second pitch goes up an easy chimney/lieback, and the awesome third pitch follows thin cracks and bolts up great face climbing to join the belay after the traverse on Dream of Wild Turkeys. While some parties use The Gobbler to pass slow parties, it is an excellent end of the day outing on its own and easily rappelled.

History

In the late 1970s, ex-Gunks climber Mike Ward moved out to Las Vegas. Early on he teamed up with George and Joanne Urioste for several new routes. The first was Arrow Place, named after an old arrowhead they found near the base. In July 1980, shortly after completing Dream of Wild Turkeys, George was back at the wall in the company of Mike Ward and Bill Bradley, to add The Gobbler variation start.

Mike recalls that it was great to climb with the Uriostes. "They had a wonderful eye for lines," he said, "and their routes are some of America's treasures." George went out of his way to make sure that the routes were bolted safely. Back at a time when bolts were placed by hand, while on the lead, George became known for his speed with the hammer. "He was very strong," Mike continues, "I remember a time at a climbers' party watching him do one-arm pull-ups while he sipped a beer with his free hand."

Climbing in Red Rocks agreed with Mike. He stayed and climbed. In 1988 he opened Desert Rock Sports, the local mountaineering shop that has provided equipment and information to an endless stream of local and visiting climbers.

– Larry DeAngelo

Strategy

Well bolted at difficult sections, there is little trick to climbing The Gobbler other than careful footwork on the first pitch. The Gobbler is yet another in the plethora of easy 5.10 routes on the Black Velvet Wall, where other parties often limit your choices to open routes. You can't really go wrong since every single route SuperTopo covers here would be the finest route at almost any other crag!

Retreat

Rappel from any pitch, but be careful not to get ropes stuck in the chimney/thin crack second pitch. A single 60m rope will get you from the second belay to the first down this crack, so if you do rap this way, coil one rope and backpack it with you while you use the other rope to rap that pitch, thereby greatly reducing the chances of a rope snag (be careful with the rope ends obviously!).

		Pitch		
The Gobbler		1	2	3
Free difficulty	≥5.10	●		●
	5.9		●	
	5.8			
	5.7			
	5.6			
	≤5.5			

A. Prince of Darkness 5.10c★★★★★ nuts: 1 set; cams: 1 ea .6-1.25", 15 draws

B. Dream of Wild Turkeys 5.10a★★★★★ nuts: 1 set; cams: 2 ea .6-1", 1 ea 1.25-3", optional 3-4" for Pitch 4; many draws

C. Yellow Brick Road 5.10b★★★★★ nuts: 2 ea med, 1 ea lrg; cams: 2 ea .6-1", 1 ea 1.25-1.5"

D. The Gobbler 5.10a★★★★ nuts: 2 ea med, 1 ea lrg; cams: 2 ea .6-1", 1 ea 1.25-1.5"

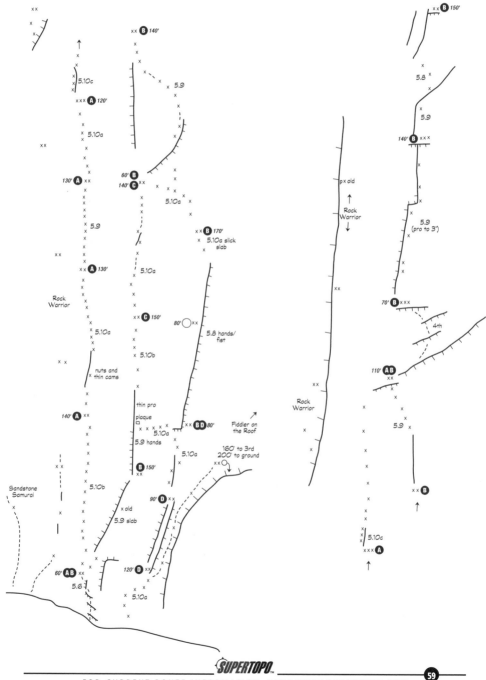

Sour Mash 5.10a★★★★

Time to climb route:	**4-5 hours**
Approach time:	**45 minutes**
Descent time:	**2 hours**
Sun exposure:	**sunrise to mid-morning**
Height of route:	**700'**

Often overlooked due to its extremely popular neighbors, Sour Mash is one of Red Rocks' finest climbs. With varied climbing, tons of thin cracks, tightly bolted face climbing cruxes, and an intriguing traversing roof to crack, Sour Mash is endless fun. To top it all off you will end the day rappelling off the middle of the giant roof!

FA: George and Joanne Urioste, 7/80.

History

Summer climbing in Red Rocks can be an interesting experience. The intense heat makes it impossible to climb in the sunshine. During their work on Sour Mash, George and Joanne set up a camp in Black Velvet Canyon. In the morning they would wake up and relax and maybe take a dip in one of the pools. Around midday, the wall would go into the shade and they would jumar to their high point. George, ever the gentleman, would go first to confirm the integrity of the fixed lines. If the climbing was hard and required much bolting, they might achieve only a single pitch before nightfall and return to camp.

The name of the route hangs on the end of a long chain. Sour Mash connects to a number of routes with whiskey themes. They all relate to "Black Velvet" which is the name of a particular brand of whiskey. Black Velvet evolved from the name "Velvet Wall" which had been chosen by Betsy Herbst to reflect the texture of the rock. But now the rest of the story... Joe Herbst and his climbing friends from the early days referred to the canyon by the code name "Crud Gulch." They worried that a name such as Velvet Canyon would sound too good and entice a flood of climbers, thus ruining the wilderness solitude that they then enjoyed.

– Larry DeAngelo

Strategy

Like most routes in Black Velvet Canyon, winter provides little sun and frigid temperatures. In spring and fall, the wall can be crowded, but Sour Mash is less popular than Prince of Darkness and Dream of Wild Turkeys, and is often free even with a late start. While Sour Mash has fewer bolts than its neighbors, most of the protection is thin.

The first pitch crux is thin and technical liebacking with tiny rounded edges—a good pair of micro-edging shoes helps. The traversing crack on the second pitch requires good footwork and is often easiest if you step below the lower crack onto small edges. The two cruxes of the fifth pitch are tricky—a good selection of thin cams combined with hidden holds can save the day. The sixth pitch has tightly bolted thin edging to a lieback crux reminiscent of Yosemite cracks, but only a few moves gain a bomber hand jam. The last pitch has a slabby crux that is easier than it looks due to good, but not obvious, edges on the left.

If you get to the top early, consider double-rope toproping some of the pitches of Fiddler on the Roof, especially the pitch above the roof, with 5.10d climbing on bullet-hard, clean brown rock with amazing horizontal thin cracks.

Retreat

Rap as shown on the topo with two ropes. If you are at the top of the second pitch, retreat will be difficult, and you may need to sacrifice a few biners on bolts to regain the first pitch. There may be other options below the traverse such as slung horns or trees, but anchors are unknown.

Sour Mash	Pitch	1	2	3	4	5	6	7
Free difficulty	≥5.10	●					●	●
	5.9			●		●		
	5.8		●					
	5.7				●			
	5.6							
	≤5.5					●		

Sour Mash 5.10a★★★★★
nuts: 1 ea micro, 2 ea sml, med, 1 ea lrg; cams: 2 ea .5-1.5", 1 ea 2-3", many quickdraws and slings

A. Overhanging Hangover 5.10a★★★★
nuts: 1 ea sml, med, lrg; cams: 1 ea .6-2"; 11 quickdraws

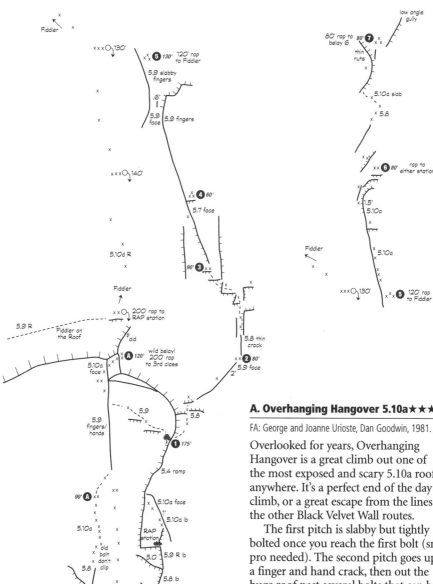

A. Overhanging Hangover 5.10a★★★★

FA: George and Joanne Urioste, Dan Goodwin, 1981.

Overlooked for years, Overhanging Hangover is a great climb out one of the most exposed and scary 5.10a roofs anywhere. It's a perfect end of the day climb, or a great escape from the lines on the other Black Velvet Wall routes.

The first pitch is slabby but tightly bolted once you reach the first bolt (small pro needed). The second pitch goes up a finger and hand crack, then out the huge roof past several bolts that can be supplemented with thin cams.

You can rap from the first pitch, from halfway up the second pitch, or from the top. Two ropes are required to rappel, and two 60m ropes are best.

Epinephrine 5.9★★★★★

Time to climb route: **6-9 hours**

Approach time: **45 minutes**

Descent time: **1-2 hours**

Sun exposure: **morning to noon**

Height of route: **2000'**

Epinephrine is one of the longest and best routes in Red Rocks and certainly one of the best 5.9 routes in the world. The ominous 600-foot-tall black chimney that forms the core of the route turns most away, especially since modern climbers often just don't have the experience needed to safely climb hard chimneys. By Yosemite Valley standards, the 5.9 chimneys on Epinephrine are "soft"—but as anyone who has climbed 5.9 chimneys in the Valley knows, they were all put up when the world's hardest routes were 5.9 and everyone climbed chimneys all the time. Slick, continuous, and serious, the chimneys on Epinephrine are not to be underestimated. Stretches with no protection can only be navigated with calm, collected movement upward, and the slippery rock can easily rattle nerves. That said, the route is beautiful, fun climbing that can go surprisingly quickly, and it offers a wide variety of climbing, grand views, and one of the largest walls that climbers without superhuman skills can ascend in a day.

History

Although Epinephrine was not climbed until 1978, the story really starts five years earlier. In 1973, Joe Herbst studied the wall and pieced together a possible route. His line followed the major chimney system to the top of the tower, then veered left to the base of the prominent ramp system. The question mark was the blank wall between the tower and the crack systems above. Joe and Jeff Lansing climbed the chimneys to have a look. The steep face above had no cracks for protection. Joe bouldered a few moves to get the feel of it. The climbing seemed doable in the 5.7 or 5.8 range, but protection was nonexistent and a fall onto the top of the tower would be a bone crusher. They descended to think things over.

A bolt or two would solve the problem, of course, but that was not Joe's way. As a strong believer in the Doug Robinson philosophy of clean climbing, Joe had climbed the entire beginning of the route hammerless. All the chimneys were done with no pitons or bolts (and, for that matter, without cams, which had not yet been invented). Joe was not about to dilute the experience by bolting the headwall. He returned to the route with Tom Kaufman on a cold day in late December. They carried one half-bag to share for the bivouac, and no pins or hammer. When they reached the top of the tower, Joe led through into unknown territory, the rope dangling uselessly from his swami belt. He reached the crack system and ledge above. It was late in the day, so they settled in to bivouac on the small ledge. The following morning they followed broken rock left and reached the base of the huge ramp. The difficulties eased, and soon they completed the first major wall in Red Rocks.

By 1978, there were some new kids in town. George and Joanne Urioste had already climbed some big routes at Red Rocks when they started looking at the Velvet Wall. Joe's original route wandered a bit, and included the easy ramp. Maybe they could do a little better. Up and slightly

Epinephrine	Pitch	1	2	3	4	5	6	7	8	9	10	11	12	13	14	15
Free difficulty	≥5.10															
	5.9			●		●		●	●		●					
	5.8	●				●	●			●						
	5.7															
	5.6		●									●				
	≤5.5											●	●	●	●	

right from the top of the tower was a clean, straight dihedral. With a little face-climbing to connect the crack systems, it would be the perfect finish for the wall. They added a face-climbing pitch off the ground to straighten out the bottom of the route, then climbed up the chimneys and headwall to Joe and Tom's bivouac ledge.

At this point they needed to bear right to gain the upper dihedral. The holds were there, but protection wasn't, so it was time to drill. With bolts for protection, they reached the dihedral. The high quality of the route was already apparent, and this precipitated a bit of a break with tradition. The prevailing ethics generally valued a highly adventurous, committed, sometimes unprotected, single push climb from ground to summit. This could involve treading some fairly dangerous ground. George and Joanne felt that such an approach would doom a great climb to obscurity, since few would be willing to take the risks. On this route, good protection was going to mean bolts. Bolts were going to mean work. Work was going to mean lots of time on the wall. The decision was made to fix ropes and put in the "route-construction" work that was necessary to make it a safe and first-rate climb.

The use of these "expedition" tactics led to an immediate rift between the Uriostes and some of the local climbers. Despite the quality of the climbing, this approach was exactly the opposite of the highly adventurous approach used by Joe Herbst just a few years previously. As it happened, the Uriostes were at work in the upper dihedral when they spotted a hiker in the streambed far below. They recognized none other than Joe Herbst out scouting additional new lines. After a shouted conversation, they invited him to join them for the upper pitches. Since Joe scouted with jumars in his pack, he was as equipped as he needed to be. Quickly united with his friends, they finished the climb together.

Although the tactics used were none that Joe would ever embrace, he agreed with their appraisal of the route as a potential classic. His opinion was high enough that

he even agreed to the placement of two additional protection bolts on the headwall and a few more in the chimneys (all of which George and Joanne had also led boltless) in order to make the route a little more accessible.

– Larry DeAngelo

Strategy

Long and continuous, Epinephrine demands an early start, usually first light. Going quick and light is the key, and most parties make the committing decision to only bring one rope (double ropes are a good idea as long as you are comfortable with keeping them flaked on hanging belays). Since nearly every anchor is bolted, and since there is little in the way of routefinding, the climbing can go very quickly. As getting stuck behind another party can cause major epics in the timing of the climb, we strongly recommend choosing to do another route if there is someone ahead of you, unless they are clearly moving fast. Many excellent routes are just 5 minutes to the left on Black Velvet Wall, and your very early start will likely leave you the choice of any route.

Skipping the first 50 feet of 5.8 by a 5.4 solo to the right is common and reduces rope-drag on the runout 5.8 friction of the upper part of the first pitch. Once entering the harder chimney pitches, the first chimney is well-protected via a 3-inch-crack in the back, and although climbing at the outside of the chimney is far easier, few leaders dare the unprotected lead. The second 5.9 chimney pitch goes up next to a large flake, past an intermediate belay, and through a scary section with somewhat loose pro to get out of the chimney to a blocky dihedral on the left. The third hard chimney section is easier due to edges on the left wall, but it is very airy and committing climbing. Above the pedestal, most find the face and dihedral climbing much more straightforward, and only a smattering of ancient 1/4" bolts and a few short runouts are to be feared. The 5.9 roof on the tenth pitch is exciting, and huge jugs on the left are the key to the roof moves.

The chimneys are often colder than expected, and when a comfortable temperature, the upper half of the climb can be hot. Climbing chimneys with bulky clothes can be hard (on the clothes as well as you), and we recommend that you check out the temperature at the base of the climb in the early morning a day ahead of time, or ask around. However, for obvious reasons, climbing chimneys in shorts and a sport top can be hard on your skin, so a balance must be struck. The climb should never be attempted in stormy or uncertain weather.

For many stronger parties, the climb goes very fast, and a great end of the day bonus is to climb Frogland, which is only 5 minutes around left from near the bottom of the descent.

Since the parking lot of Black Velvet Canyon is not in the loop, most parties drive in very early and hike up. Bivying at the base of the wall is not advisable, since it would be a pain to return and get bivy gear.

Retreat

Retreat from any pitch by rappelling with two ropes from bolts, except the pitch above the pedestal, where you can sling the tree. Most anchors have fixed rap rings. Rappelling is not advised above the Black Tower, since it is common for ropes to snag.

There are many places to bivy along the descent (and a few on the 4th class ramp up top), and of course headlamps and a lighter are always a good idea on any long route.

Laura Snider looking very relaxed in the second chimney.

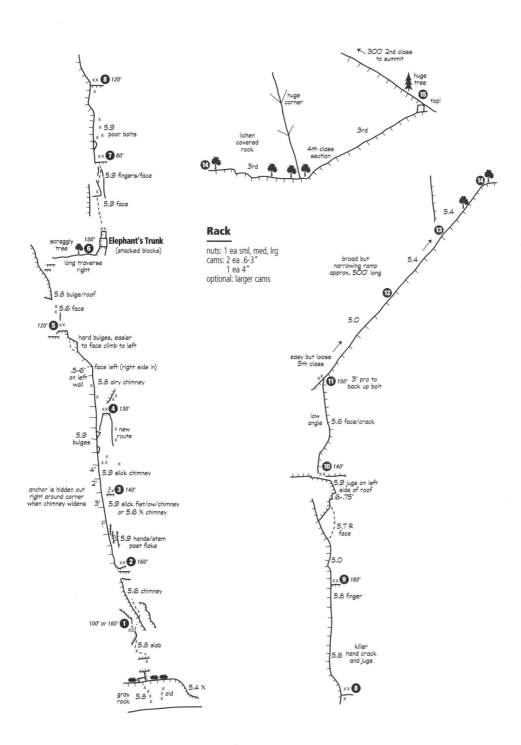

xx **8** 120'
x

x
x 5.9
x x poor bolts
xx **7** 80'

5.9 fingers/face

x 5.9 face

xx
scraggly 150' **Elephant's Trunk**
tree **6** (stacked blocks)
long traverse
right

5.8 bulge/roof

x 5.6 face
x
120' **5** xx
hard bulges, easier
to face climb to left

.5-6" face left (right side in)
on left
wall x 5.8 airy chimney
x
xx **4** 130'

5.9 x new
bulges route

x
xx
4" 5.9 slick chimney
2"
xx **3** 140' x
anchor is hidden out
right around corner 3" 5.9 slick fist/ow/chimney
when chimney widens or 5.6 X chimney

5.9 hands/stem
past flake

xx **2** 160'

5.6 chimney

100' or 160' **1**
xx
5.8 slab
x
x

gray 5.8 x x old 5.4 X
rock x x
x

Rack

nuts: 1 ea sml, med, lrg
cams: 2 ea .6-3"
       1 ea 4"
optional: larger cams

← 300' 2nd class
to summit

huge
tree
huge **15** top!
corner
lichen 3rd
covered 4th class
rock section
14 3rd **14**

5.4
broad but **13**
narrowing ramp
5.4 approx. 500' long 5.4
12

5.0
easy but loose
5th class
xx **11** 150' 3" pro to
back up bolt

low
angle 5.6 face/crack

10 140'
xx
5.9 jugs on left
side of roof
.6-.75"

x 5.7 R
face

5.0

xx **9** 160'

5.8 finger

killer
5.6 hand crack
and jugs
xx **8**
x

Burlap Buttress, East Formation

Arrow Place

Greg Barnes

The Burlap Buttress is an obvious, dark formation in the sun opposite Frogland, and many climbers shivering in the shade have wondered why they are not across the canyon in the sun. There are actually two entirely separate formations called "Burlap Buttress," one of which is much closer to the parking area (the east formation), and one of which is more triangular and faces the Black Velvet Wall (the west formation). Black rock with incut edges, topped with white rock of poor quality, Burlap Buttress is nowhere near as huge and impressive as the shady walls across the canyon, but it is still larger and steeper than it appears at first.

Approach

Hike up the approach trail for Black Velvet (see page 39) until it first encounters the edge of the wash. A trail drops down here (one alternate for the main Black Velvet approach). Follow this trail down into the wash, hike up the wash for about 50 yards past the worst of the oak trees, and then follow burro trails up the far side of the wash. Head up to the wall via burro trails and easy hiking; beware of cacti.

Descent

Reverse the easy hike back to the car.

Arrow Place 5.9★★★★

Time to climb route: **1-2 hours**

Approach time: **30 minutes**

Descent time: **45 minutes to 1 hour**

Sun exposure: **sunrise to afternoon**

Height of route: **400'**

Arrow Place is an excellent climb, with steep stemming, face, and hand cracks on black rock. It is fairly short, but the added attractions of sunny exposure and fewer crowds are incentives to climb this route. It is neighbored by other older traditional routes, and for an adventure, check out these lines using the written descriptions in the newly reprinted Urioste guide.

FA: Dick Tonkin, George Urioste, Mike Ward, 5/79.

History

The name of this route stems from the nicely crafted Indian arrowhead that the first ascent party found at the top of the first pitch. They speculated that an ancient hunter took a shot at a bird and was unable to retrieve his arrow.

This route is notable as it was the first of many first ascents in which Mike Ward participated in the company of the Uriostes. Mike came to Las Vegas in 1975 to deliver a car to his brother—he never left.

As a Gunks climber, Mike was familiar with the New Paltz mountaineering shop run by the famous Dick Williams. Mike thought it was a "really great store," and was inspired. In 1988 he opened Desert Rock Sports, which has since become a focal point for Las Vegas climbing. In the mid-1990s the store received a visit from none other than Dick Williams in the company of fellow east coast luminaries Jim McCarthy and Rich Goldstone. Mike had the pleasure of telling Dick that he himself had provided the original inspiration.

– Larry DeAngelo

Strategy

With a short approach, relatively short pitches, and easy hiking, Arrow Place can be done at the start or end of a longer day in Black Velvet, or on its own at a relaxed pace.

A crux section of tricky 5.9 climbing is right off the deck, with the unappetizing prospect of landing in a big Yucca plant. Very thin pro protects this, and it is wise to place several pieces, especially as the "obvious" placement rejects nuts and a thin cam is hard to get in. This is one of the few free climbs where those who own Lowe Balls should definitely bring them. The stemming crux at the top of the first pitch is well-protected by cams and nuts, but it's a good idea to do some stretching ahead of time.

The fourth and fifth pitches are loose and not recommended.

Frogland and the many excellent climbs of Whiskey Peak are just across the canyon, and the big routes of Black Velvet are a short hike up canyon.

Retreat

Rappel the route with one 70m rope or two ropes.

Arrow Place		Pitch 1	2	3
Free difficulty	≥5.10			
	5.9	●		
	5.8		●	
	5.7			●
	5.6			
	≤5.5			

Rack

nuts: 1 set
cams: 1 ea .33"
    2 ea .4-.5"
    1 ea .6-1.5", 3-4"
    3 ea 2"
optional: thin Lowe Balls to protect start

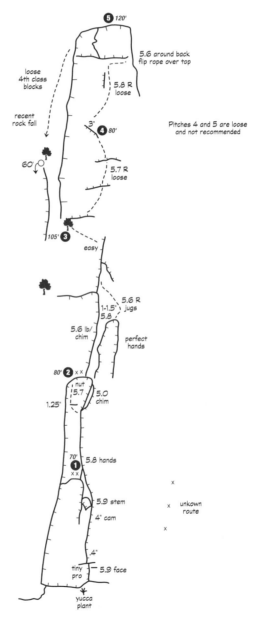

5 120'

5.6 around back
flip rope over top

loose
4th class
blocks

5.8 R
loose

4 80'   3"

recent
rock fall

Pitches 4 and 5 are loose
and not recommended

60'   O

5.7 R
loose

105' **3**

easy

5.6 R
jugs

1-1.5"
5.8

5.6 lb/
chim

perfect
hands

80' **2** x x

nut
5.7   5.0
chim

1.25"

70' **1**   5.8 hands
x x

x

5.9 stem

x   unkown
route

4" cam

x

.4"

tiny
pro   5.9 face

yucca
plant

First Creek Canyon

The climbing areas in First Creek Canyon are at the mouth of the canyon and easily located. The only thing in the way is the long straight approach from the highway. Since you approach from the highway, there's no need to worry about the Loop Road hours. Lotta Balls and the Alcohol Wall are usually shaded, with only the Romper Room area getting sun, so they are best in warmer weather.

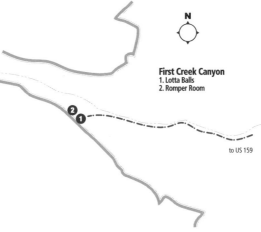

First Creek Canyon
1. Lotta Balls
2. Romper Room

to US 159

Sarah Felchlin

Lotta Balls Wall
Alcohol Wall

Approach time: 1 hour

Sun exposure: early morning to noon

Height of routes: 80' to 600'

Larry DeAngelo

The Lotta Balls area is full of clean cracks and steep dihedrals on excellent dark brown rock. Located at the base of a huge slabby mountainside, the cliff has a middle section of harder climbs on super-slick grey rock (the Alcohol Wall), and a preponderance of brown knobs/balls sticking out of the rock (where Lotta Balls gets its name). With Lotta Balls plus steep and easier one-pitch cracks on the far right, the crag is very popular.

Usually shaded, Lotta Balls gets only early morning sun, but as the crag is right at the mouth of the canyon it can be warm. Also, the routes on the far right get sun for a lot longer. Because of this, in cooler weather it'd be best to warm up on Doobie Dance and Romper Room before climbing Lotta Balls, but you run the risk of others getting ahead on this popular 5.8.

Approach

With a long approach, First Creek Canyon is paradoxically one of the easiest approaches for the canyons of Red Rocks. While it is a long walk, it is on an old, flat jeep road for most of the way, with only a few sections of sandy wash bottom to slow you down. Since the trailhead for First Creek is outside the Loop Road, and since the climbs are mostly short with simple rappels, climbing in First Creek Canyon is among the most flexible in Red Rocks.

Descent

Rappel most routes and reverse the approach.

A. Lotta Balls   5.8★★★★★

FA: Betsy and Joe Herbst, Randal Grandstaff, Tom Kaufman, 3/77.

The classic of the area, Lotta Balls was a scary face in the pre-sticky rubber days.

Randy Grandstaff drilled the 1/4" bolt in 1977 while standing on small knobs, and amazingly it was not replaced until 25 years later! While modern sticky rubber may make the moves easier, it is still an intimidating lead for the 5.8 leader. Killer crack and flake climbing, the namesake knobby face, and a cool dihedral are the highlights. Many people rappel off the top of the second pitch to avoid the walk-off, which, while fairly short, has 3 short rappels, some 4th class scrambling, and brush, trees, and loose rock.

History

The first ascent of this route was accomplished in March 1977 by Joe and Betsy Herbst, Tom Kaufman, and Randal Grandstaff. This was an impressive assembly of the first wave of Red Rocks pioneers. Joe Herbst was the granddaddy of modern Red Rocks climbing. Most conspicuous for his first ascents of the original "big three" walls (Rainbow, Velvet, and Aeolian), he was also the driving force behind a spectacular array of long free climbs and high quality crag routes. With his quiet competence and strict clean climbing ethic, he became a role model and inspiration for the emerging generation of locals who would carry Red

Rocks climbing into the future.

Randal Grandstaff was the first of that new generation. He was a young teenager in the early 1970s when he befriended Joe, who was only a few years older. A few years can mean a big difference to an enthusiastic 14 year old with a passion to climb. Joe's experience (he had been to Yosemite and climbed El Cap!) represented the goal toward which young Randal aspired.

Tom Kaufman was not a local Las Vegas resident, but his close friendship with Joe meant frequent visits and many climbs. If you leaf through the first ascent list in the back of Joanne Urioste's original 1984 guidebook, you will see many references to "Joe Herbst and a friend." It's a pretty good bet that the "friend" was Tom Kaufman. One of the main sources of information for the guide was Joe's notebook where he recorded his first ascents. The entry was usually signed by the participants. As a young M.D., Tom had already perfected the illegible scrawl for which his profession is famous. His signature was thus generally unidentifiable when Joanne was compiling the guidebook following Joe's withdrawal from climbing several years later.

On the first ascent the quartet had an easy time with the clean crack and flake of the first pitch. Above them lay the "surreal" face dotted with numerous spherical protrusions of uncertain security. Joe led the initial fifteen feet of pitch two, and drilled one of his infrequent bolts from a small dished out stance. The difficulties increased above. "The real credit has to go to Randy," says Joe. "He's the one who stood on those little marbles above my crummy bolt and drilled a good one to protect the tough moves." Tom coined the name for the route based on his dire predictions of the effect of the protruding knobs on the anatomy of a climber taking a slider off the crux.

– *Larry DeAngelo*

B. Gin Ricky   5.10c★★★

FA: Richard Harrison, Paul Crawford, Paul Van Betten, Sal Mamusia, Paul "Obi" Obenheim, 1983.

A long endurance dihedral crack which requires two 55m or longer ropes to descend, Gin Ricky is clean, beautiful, and one of the longer pitches of its grade in Red Rocks.

The approach to Lotta Balls and Alcohol Wall. 1. Lotta Balls 2. Romper Room

C. Rob Roy 5.10a R★★★★

FA: Richard Harrison, Paul Crawford, Paul Van Betten, Sal Mamusia, Paul "Obi" Obenheim, 1983.

Rob Roy is a clean climb on slick rock, with many tricky slab sections. Unfortunately, it is too runout for most people; if leading, the belayer should do a careful job spotting the leader until they get to the first bolt. You can toprope this climb with two ropes by climbing the Friendship Route.

D. Mai Tai 5.10d R★★★★

FA: Richard Harrison, Paul Van Betten, Sal Mamusia, Paul "Obi" Obenheim, 1983.

An awesome route up a slick dihedral with roofs at the start, Mai Tai is a must-do if you are a very confident leader or if you climb the Friendship Route and set a toprope. The crux, which is a combination of very thin face, tips lieback, and stemming on slippery rock, is poorly protected for the leader. At the top of the dihedral, the route goes right and a bit down to join the first pitch anchor of Friendship Route. However, if toproping from the anchor of Rob Roy, you should clip a bolt as a directional and have the last climber do a controlled pendulum/tension traverse back to the left.

E. Friendship Route 5.10a★★

FA: Joe Herbst and friends, 1988.

The intimidating clean but wide section on the first pitch scares many away. The climbing, a combination of liebacking, stemming, and offwidth techniques, is not hard, but it is hard to protect well without large gear. The second pitch is a short dihedral/stem problem on dirty rock and is quite challenging. (Luckily, the 1/4" bolts were just replaced.) Walk left on the large ledge/ramp to rappel off the anchors of Rob Roy, being careful not to dislodge the many large loose rocks. The main reason to climb the second pitch is to set a double-rope toprope on the excellent climbs to the left.

F. Doobie Dance 5.6★★★★

FA: Unknown, late 1970s.

While short, Doobie Dance is killer climbing up finger cracks, plates, and edges to a rap anchor. The steep brown wall looks way harder than 5.6, but more jugs and finger locks are always within reach. A bit of loose rock and hollow pro, plus the steep wall, make this challenging for the 5.6 leader.

G. Romper Room 5.7★★★★

FA: Unknown, late 1970s.

While looking similar to its neighbor, Romper Room is predominantly flakes and liebacking and is a super fun climb. Unfortunately, due to the somewhat hollow flakes, the protection is not always solid, therefore it is not the best lead if you are pushing your limits. It is possible to climb right from the anchor of Doobie Dance to gain the anchor of Romper Room and set a toprope, but only do this if other parties are not doing Romper Room!

Larry DeAngelo leading the roof on the first pitch of Lotta Balls.

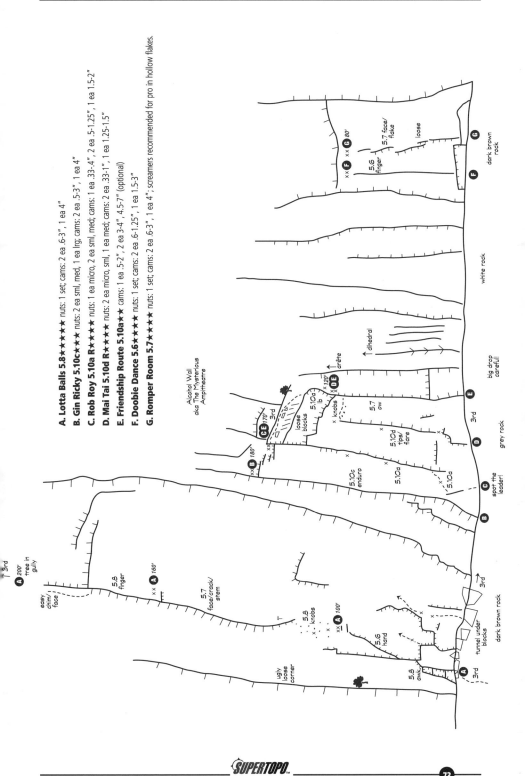

A. Lotta Balls 5.8 ★★★★★ nuts: 1 set; cams: 2 ea .6-3", 1 ea 4"

B. Gin Ricky 5.10c ★★★ nuts: 2 ea sml, med, 1 ea lrg; cams: 2 ea .5-3", 1 ea 4"

C. Rob Roy 5.10a R ★★★★★ nuts: 1 ea micro, 2 ea sml, med; cams: 1 ea .33-.4", 2 ea .5-1.25", 1 ea 1.5-2"

D. Mai Tai 5.10d R ★★★★★ nuts: 2 ea micro, sml, 1 ea med; cams: 2 ea .33-1", 1 ea 1.25-1.5"

E. Friendship Route 5.10a ★ cams: 1 ea .5-2", 2 ea 3-4", 4.5-7" (optional)

F. Doobie Dance 5.6 ★★★★★ nuts: 1 set; cams: 2 ea .6-1.25", 1 ea 1.5-3"

G. Romper Room 5.7 ★★★ nuts: 1 set; cams: 2 ea .6-3", 1 ea 4"; screamers recommended for pro in hollow flakes.

Oak Creek Canyon

Sarah Felchlin

Huge, complex, and varied, Oak Creek Canyon has some of the warmest climbs in the main canyons of Red Rocks. South-facing routes where the sun is not blocked by the opposite wall of the canyon often get uncomfortably warm, and are perfect for cooler days. Long approaches, long routes, and short Loop Road hours often force climbers into choosing to hike an extra half hour from the old Oak Creek Campground on Highway 159, although the Oak Creek trailhead (last stop on the Loop Road) is closer. Oak Creek Canyon routes are some of the warmest longer routes and are best in late fall through early spring.

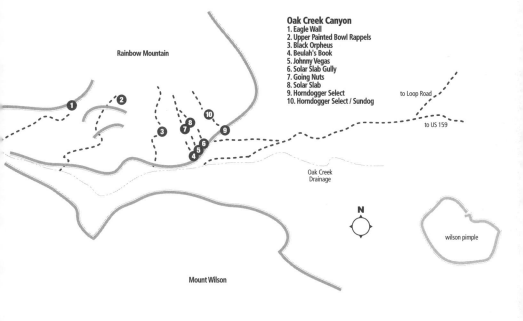

Oak Creek Canyon
1. Eagle Wall
2. Upper Painted Bowl Rappels
3. Black Orpheus
4. Beulah's Book
5. Johnny Vegas
6. Solar Slab Gully
7. Going Nuts
8. Solar Slab
9. Horndogger Select
10. Horndogger Select / Sundog

Shelly Presson Dunbar plans her next move on Pitch 5 of Levitation 29. (Greg Epperson)

Eagle Wall

Hidden far back in Oak Creek Canyon, the immense and beautiful Eagle Wall is not easily seen without a big hike. As you approach the wall, its size is obscured by an intervening shoulder, and it's not until you stand at the base that you realize just how big the wall is. The featured brown rock, straight crack systems, and endless face fade upward into the sky on a wall that seems endless when you are on it. The name partly comes from a rough shape of a flying eagle made of brown varnish on the largely white middle to upper part of the wall.

Approach

The approach to the Eagle Wall is straightforward, but extremely long because most of it involves scrambling over boulders. Hike the trail to the Solar Slab area and dive down into the canyon bottom when the bench ends about 200 yards past Solar Slab. Hike up the canyon, then up the north fork when the canyon divides. This is the only place you could get off route, so keep an eye out for the north fork/south fork split. Head up the north fork for a long while, looking for two HUGE pine trees in the middle of the drainage. From the right (north) tree, head up slick 3rd class slabs, and contour right along the easiest way up the slabs. After about 20 minutes you'll reach the main wall and downclimb a 60-foot 3rd/4th class gully, then continue up for 5 minutes to the base of the Eagle Wall. Eagle Dance starts in a small black dihedral about 50 feet right of a large detached pillar. Levitation 29 starts 50 feet right of Eagle Dance, with a few bolts visible not far off the deck, and heads through a roof 150 feet up. Ringtail starts 100 yards right of Levitation 29 in left-angling cracks about 50 feet before the huge drop off into the Painted Bowl.

Descent

Eagle Dance
We recommend that you rappel the route. A final pitch of low-angle crack to face with four old bolts leads to the top, and a LONG journey up canyon and back down the drainage will take most people who have not done it in the range of 4 or more hours.

Levitation 29
Rap the route with two ropes from the top of Pitch 9, or continue (30 feet of 5.6) to the top and walk off west, then all the way down the canyon. Rapping the route will take most people 1-1.5 hours or so; reversing the approach will take in the range of 1.5-2.5 hours depending on which route you take and how fast you hike.

Ringtail
Rap the route with two ropes, or continue up Rainbow Buttress to the top and walk off. The rappels take about 30 minutes.

Eagle Dance 5.10c A0★★★★

Time to climb route: **4-6 hours**

Approach time: **2-3 hours**

Descent time: **3-4 hours**

Sun exposure: **mid-morning to evening**

Height of route: **1000'**

Eagle Wall is home to one of Red Rocks' most celebrated routes, Levitation 29 (5.11). Yet the fame of Levitation 29 has left its awesome neighbor Eagle Dance surprisingly vacant. Long, sustained, and beautiful, Eagle Dance had the unfortunate reputation of a death route due to the terrible bolts. Luckily, the ASCA replaced 72 bolts on the route in 2002, and it is now in prime shape. Nearly every pitch is 5.10 with a variety of climbing from thin crack to sustained edging face. Parts feel like a sport climb with up to 13 bolts on a single pitch, yet a loose and challenging 5.10a pitch followed by an overhung traversing bolt ladder through an airy roof give a distinct big wall feel. Eagle Dance is long, unique, and rewarding.

History

George and Joanne Urioste started work on this route in early 1980. Because of the amount of work required, the route was climbed with fixed ropes leading upward from the Urioste's "Eagle Camp," a level spot at the base of the route. Keeping the camp stocked was a major effort in itself, requiring many trips up the rocky streambed of Oak Creek. Joanne reports that they memorized every boulder on their numerous trips, frequently done in the dark and with no headlamps.

Back in the late 1970s, the cliffs of Red Rocks were frequented by some very large soaring birds. Though there was speculation that they might have been condors (due to their impressive size), the local climbers referred to them generically as eagles. One such bird kept the Uriostes company, hovering continuously over Oak Creek and Mount Wilson to the south. As George and Joanne were working on one of the lower pitches on the route, they accidentally dropped a baby angle piton. While it was not a critical loss, no climber gives up gear without a fight, so that afternoon they scoured the brushy area at the base of the route. After searching with no result, they were about to give up. With hope waning, Joanne suggested that perhaps they should ask the eagle for guidance—and they found the piton less than a minute later! And so the route and wall were named after the charmed bird. It was only later, while studying the wall from a distance, that they noticed a peculiar patch of dark varnish high on the face. Its outline, in the shape of a westbound eagle, made the omen complete.

A year or two earlier, local pioneer Joe Herbst had had his own eagle experience. Back in the canyons, Joe had scouted an interesting crack line. The climbing looked good, so Joe planned a first ascent attempt during the upcoming visit of his friend Andre Langenbacher (with whom Joe also climbed Unfinished Symphony). The climb would go up steep cracks to a wide point, with the apparent crux being a spectacular jam out the roof of the cave-like opening. They climbed a few pitches and found that the route was living up to their high expectations. A few hundred feet up, they climbed into the alcove beneath

Eagle Dance		Pitch 1	2	3	4	5	6	7	8	9	10
Free difficulty	≥5.10			●	●	●	●	●	●	●	
	5.9	●									●
	5.8		●								
	5.7										
	5.6										
	≤5.5										

the looming overhang. However, their anticipated belay spot was occupied by a huge nest. It was the size of a bathtub, made of sticks and twigs, and littered with small rodent skulls and a few grayish brown feathers. A hurried discussion led to agreement that the route would have to be abandoned and unrecorded, lest additional climber traffic further disturb the nesting site. It may have been this very eagle, showing his appreciation, that guided the Uriostes to their lost piton on the Eagle Wall.

– Larry DeAngelo

Strategy

Eagle Wall is in full sunlight for most of the day, and thus can get quite warm. However, due to the long approach, the shorter days of late fall or early spring are often just not long enough for most people to complete the route. Thus, an early start and fast progress are strongly recommended. Only a light rack is needed, plus a lot of draws, and some aiders. Double ropes are definitely recommended in order to rappel without extra weight—and they come in handy on a couple of pitches with winding protection.

The slick, black start of Eagle Dance.

Greg Barnes

Care should be taken right off the ground, since while the climbing is only 5.8, the black rock is slick and there is no protection for the first bit. On upper pitches nearly every crux is right above a bomber bolt, and only when the 5.10a flake pitch comes does a serious feel intrude on the climbing. Here, loose flakes plus hollow pro grab your attention until reaching the bolts in the crux section. Care must be taken in order to avoid dropping any rocks on this pitch. The bolt ladder is strenuous, and a pair of ultralight aiders is recommended for the leader and the follower, although girth-hitched slings are another option. The last few pitches are surprisingly slabby and require careful attention to footwork.

Sun is the biggest threat on the climb—it can be surprisingly hot on the wall and a lack of adequate water can cause problems. Inclement weather is not to be taken lightly as Eagle Dance is far up the canyon and it often snows even when the weather seems warm right before a storm.

If you finish early, consider trying the first few pitches of Levitation 29, just 150 feet to the right. The first is 5.10b with some pro and a few bolts up small, tricky, angular dihedrals. The second has excellent 5.10d stemming and edging to a wild overhung flake to face (5.11b). Ringtail is just right of Levitation 29 and is another excellent option.

The cave just to the right of the fourth/ fifth pitch used to be home to Peregrine falcons, and if they do return, they would definitely pose a threat to climbers because of their tendency to attack people near nests. However, if they do return, the climbing rangers would likely close the route until the young were fledged that year. If you do get on the route and see raptor activity in that cave, descend immediately and inform the climbing rangers.

Retreat

Rap from any pitch with two ropes. You cannot rap or lower from the top of the bolt ladder pitch to the base of that pitch, but it is easy to rap to the pitch before that (only 50 feet lower).

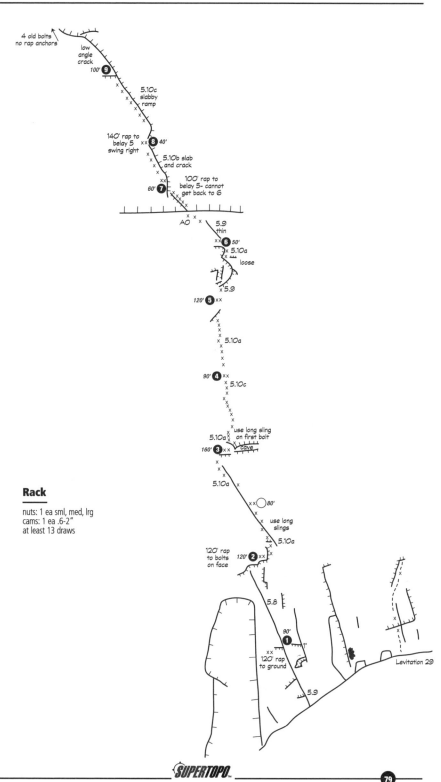

Rack

nuts: 1 ea sml, med, lrg
cams: 1 ea .6-2"
at least 13 draws

Levitation 29 5.11c★★★★★

Time to climb route: **4-7 hours**	
Approach time: **2-3 hours**	
Descent time: **1.5-2.5 hours**	
Sun exposure: **all day**	
Height of route: **1000'**	

Levitation 29 has long been named Red Rock's best climb. Stellar and varied climbing up a deceptively long but sometimes vague crack system, Levitation 29 is impressive and intimidating. Starting over 1,000 feet above the desert, and near a drop-off into the Painted Bowl, Levitation quickly takes on major exposure with Las Vegas spread far below.

FA: George and Joanne Urioste, Bill Bradley, 4/81.
FFA: Lynn Hill, John Long, Joanne Urioste, 5/81.

History

Levitation 29 on the Eagle Wall is the Uriostes' ultimate route. On the first ascent, George led the difficult sections, using aid when necessary. Joanne was able to follow it free, rising buoyantly on one of those "low-gravity" days. Since the route was completed on her 29th birthday, it earned the name "Levitation 29."

Due to Joanne's efforts, they knew the route would go free; all that was required was a strong team to make a clean lead of it. As it happened, John Long and Lynn Hill were in town and living for the time at Randy Grandstaff's rambling ranch house that during its era was something of a climbers' nerve center. An invitation was extended and a plan was made. John and Lynn would join Joanne for the free ascent, while George would jumar the fixed ropes and take photographs. With a team of such high caliber, the free ascent was accomplished with no problems. The quality of the climbing was so high that this route became Lynn Hill's selection in Mark Krause's book *50 Favorite Climbs*, which ironically left out Joanne's name as a member of the FFA team.

There is a further irony. Each time that George has climbed the route since, there has been some activity to distract him from a pure free climbing effort. He is either drilling the bolts, or taking the photos, or cleaning the fixed ropes, or most recently, replacing the old bolts with new strong ones. So, although there is probably no other climber that has expended more energy on the route than George, he has not yet climbed the route free!

– Larry DeAngelo

Strategy

Lines are common at Levitation, even with the high grade and long approach. Start very early (needed anyway for most people to complete the route even without lines), and if you get stuck behind a slow party, jump on Eagle Dance or Ringtail. The first few pitches of Eagle Dance and Ringtail are excellent, easily rappelled, and offer a variety of challenges. All of these routes can be done with a light rack and a bunch of draws.

Despite the grade, the climb is a bolt ladder at most crux sections, and the steep nature of the cruxes make it a safe climb to whip on. However, the crux pitch is enduro, and those not leading to 5.11c will have trouble despite the many bolts. The last three pitches—including a burly 5.10d—are on slopey white rock of mediocre quality, and the lower angle makes falls more dangerous.

Levitation 29		Pitch 1	2	3	4	5	6	7	8	9
Free difficulty	5.11	●				●	●			
	5.10	●			●			●	●	
	5.9									●
	5.8		●							
	5.7									
	≤5.6									

SUPERTOPO

Strong leaders can skip bolts on the crux pitch and link it with the sixth pitch for an incredible 160 feet of overhung climbing.

Eagle Wall can get very hot on warmer days, and Black Velvet Canyon is a good alternative (for a route of comparable difficulty, try Only the Good Die Young). After a storm, the canyon bottom in Oak Creek can have a lot of pools, and so it's a good idea to wait a few days (and it's a bad idea to crank on Levitation if the holds haven't thoroughly dried).

Bivy permits can be obtained for Levitation 29, and are not a bad idea, although the added weight of the gear, plus the lack of the water at the base, make bivying a major haul. You can get permits from the climbing rangers through the Late Exit permit system at 702-515-5050. A Late Exit Pass should always be secured for long routes such as Levitation 29 (unless you hike from the highway).

Retreat

Rappel. You will need two ropes for the rap from Pitch 3, although most other raps can be done with a single 60m rope.

René Vitins leading the crux of Levitation 29.

Greg Barnes

Rack
___
nuts: 1 set
cams: 1 ea .6-1.5″ (optional 3″)
13 quickdraws

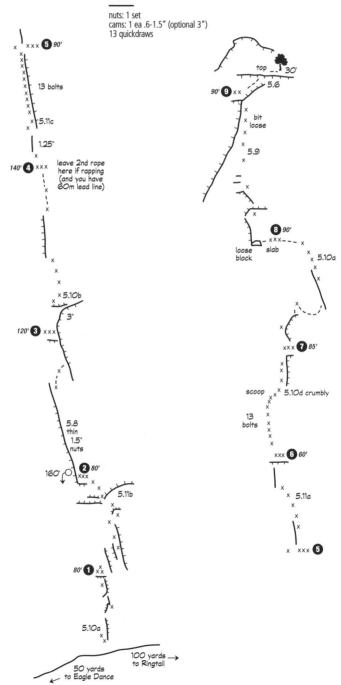

x x x x ⑤ *90'*
x
x
x
13 bolts
x
x
x
x
x x 5.11c
x

1.25″
x
140' ④ x x x
leave 2nd rope
here if rapping
(and you have
60m lead line)
x

x

x 5.10b
x
3″
120' ③ x x x

x

5.8
thin
1.5″
nuts

160' ○ ② *80'*
x x x   x
x
x x 5.11b
x x
x
x
x x
80' ① x x
x
x

5.10a
x
x

50 yards
← to Eagle Dance

100 yards →
to Ringtail

x
top __ 🌳 *30'*
5.6
90' ⑨ x x
x
bit
loose
x
5.9
x

x
⑧ *90'*
x x x — — — x
loose   slab   x
block   x 5.10a
x

x
x
x x x ⑦ *85'*
x
x
x
scoop x x 5.10d crumbly
x x
13   x
bolts x
x
x
x x x ⑥ *60'*

x 5.11a
x
x
x
x x x x ⑤

Roxanna Brock starts up Pitch 8 of Levitation 29. (Greg Epperson)

Ringtail 5.10d★★★

Time to climb route: **2-3 hours**

Approach time: **2-3 hours**

Descent time: **2-3 hours**

Sun exposure: **all day**

Height of route: **1000'**

Ringtail joins the moderate Rainbow Buttress route which climbs the right side of the huge Black Tower. It is unlike the other climbs on Eagle Wall, with awkward crack and corner climbing, stemming, and a very thin edge crux traverse on a steep slab. The climbing is reminiscent of the technical faces and corner climbs of Black Velvet Canyon.

FA: George and Joanne Urioste, 1/81.

History

With their experience on Eagle Dance the previous year, the Uriostes knew there was great potential on the Eagle Wall. They restocked their high camp and went to work on a new route on the far right side of the cliff. They returned in the evenings to spend the night in their tent. The nights, however, were not a restful as they had hoped. It seems that the top area of the ramp was inhabited by a ringtail cat with a playful streak. His primary form of recreation was to jump onto the side of the tent, slide down, then scamper around and do it again. The larcenous little beast later stole George's Swiss army knife.

– Larry DeAngelo

Strategy

Like the other Eagle Wall routes, Ringtail is a long ways in. Thankfully, the southern exposure means that it is one of the few

longer routes that is fine during mid-winter (the first ascent was in January!). Ringtail is also fairly short (unless combined with Rainbow Buttress), so an early start is not mandatory. However, with all the great climbing, it is not at all unreasonable to climb Ringtail and the first half of Eagle Dance or Levitation 29 in a short winter day. Ringtail requires more pro than its neighbors, but still only a light rack.

The second pitch is unquestionably the crux. Originally rated 5.10, the crux has seemed stiff to most people, and in November 2002 George Urioste admitted it's "probably a bona fide 5.11a." Fun 5.10 face climbing on somewhat loose edges leads up 40 feet from the belay past four bolts. The difficulties are obvious with a 20-foot traverse left on very thin holds, and in the middle, no feet at all except smears on tiny undulations in the smooth black rock. With the newly replaced bolts there's nothing to fear and nothing to hit if you fall, so it's a fun bouldering challenge.

Getting off the belay at the start of the third pitch is fairly tricky. Because there's no way to get pro and the holds are somewhat suspect, care should be taken.

The fifth pitch is somewhat intimidating, and climbs pretty much how it looks from the belay. A tight flared corner (small nuts protect the crux) and flared chimney technique is how to climb it (no face holds to use this time). It's a good pitch, steep and well-protected, and it can be refreshing to climb something that requires a bit of grunting after all the face climbing at Red Rocks. If it's not your cup of tea, it's easy to rappel before the last pitch.

From partway up the fourth pitch, steep thin cracks lead up and left to a bolted belay and some great bolted face climbing. This route, "Mountain Beast," goes all the way to the top and is described in Joanne Urioste's 2003 Red Book Supplement.

Bivi permits can be obtained for this wall using the Late Exit permit line.

Retreat

Rappel the route with two ropes.

Ringtail		Pitch				
		1	2	3	4	5
Free difficulty	≥5.10		●	●		
	5.9	●			●	●
	5.8					
	5.7					
	5.6					
	≤5.5					

Rack

nuts: 1 set
cams: 1 ea .6-3"

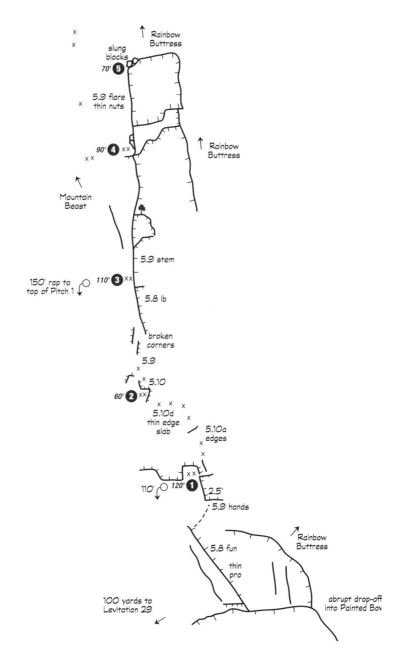

Black Orpheus Buttress

The steep, broken Black Orpheus Buttress hosts one of the best moderate routes in Red Rocks. This brown wall, actually the southwest face of Solar Slab Wall, is totally out of sight on the approach. With a long approach and descent, plus lack of easy retreat, the Black Orpheus Buttress hosts one of the more committing moderate routes at Red Rocks.

Greg Barnes

Approach

Oak Creek Canyon is at the very end of the loop road. Because of this, you can also park at the old Oak Creek Campground along the main highway and avoid the hassle of the Loop Road, at the price of an extra 20-30 minute hike in each direction.

Black Orpheus is around the corner from Solar Slab, but the boulder-strewn canyon bottom and the long 3rd and 4th class approach takes about 2 hours. Hike past Solar Slab, then drop into the canyon bottom. Hike up the canyon for about 1/4 mile, looking for a cairn on top of a white boulder on the right. Black Orpheus starts well above the canyon floor after a series of slabs and bushy areas and is not obvious from the bottom of the canyon, so examine the SuperTopo picture to help you determine where to head up. The pile of rocks on the white boulder is just as the canyon bottom takes a vague curve to the left, and is well before the split in the canyon. Depending on exactly where you go up, you must negotiate usually at least one 4th class band of 40-foot cliffs, and some may want to rope up for these sections.

Once you reach the wall, Black Orpheus begins in the largest left-facing dihedral; to the left is slick polished rock and some bushes 40 feet up on a ledge.

Descent

Four descents are possible. Most people use one of the two Upper Painted Bowl descents, but you can also downclimb to the rappels for Solar Slab, or rap the long Upper Solar Slab Gully. We only describe the Upper Painted Bowl descents here; the Solar Slab descents should not be used unless familiar with them, and even then they often have other parties clogging them. **None of these descents should be attempted in the dark without someone who knows the descent.** It is far better to scramble up to wide flat ledges with bushes and bivy for the night.

Greg Barnes

View of Black Orpheus from the approach.

SUPERTOPO

Upper Painted Bowl double-rope descent
From the top of Black Orpheus, hike up slabs for a short distance (50-100 yards) to a large ledge which heads around left. Hike along this ledge around the corner, where you will see the ledge descending steeply behind a huge flake. Scramble down behind this flake to a ledge/platform with bolts at the far end. From these bolts, rappel 130 feet, passing an intermediate rappel station, to a set of bolts. From here it is 165 feet to 3rd class slabs. As of spring 2002, there is NO intermediate station allowing a rappel with only one rope.

Once you reach the slabs you are in the upper region of the Lower Painted Bowl. Scramble down long 2nd and 3rd class slabs, staying on the right side of the bowl, aiming for a shoulder on the right with a prominent large rounded boulder. Here, turn the corner to the right and head down and traverse right along another long 2nd and 3rd class slab below a headwall. When the slab hits a line of bushes and forces you down, it seems logical to keep traversing. However, keep heading down and left on the only ledge system, finding abundant cairns along the way. After 200 yards, the ledge system ends in a steep slab, with bushes heading left. Here, you go down steep 3rd/4th class slabs for about 100 yards, then contour right above a line of bushes for 50 yards. Then you head down 3rd and 4th class blocks until just above the streambed; a very slick traverse to the right, or sliding down on your butt, gets you down this final 30 feet. Always head right at this very end section, or a drop-off is encountered.

Once down in the streambed, it takes most people about an hour and a half to get back to the trailhead. The entire descent takes approximately 3 hours for people who make no mistakes or have to backtrack.

Upper Painted Bowl single-rope descent:
From the top of Black Orpheus, hike up slabs for about 400 yards, aiming for a colored headwall. Just before getting to the obviously 5th class headwall, pass through a cool little arch, then head left along the base of the wall. After 100 yards, slide/chimney down a 4th class gully/chimney leading to large trees—be very careful on the slick rock. From here, work down into the Upper Painted Bowl (Chicken Lips, a long 5.10 route, starts on your right). When you can see the whole Upper Painted Bowl, head down and aim for bushes on the left—behind them is a gully that you will rap down. It may take a bit of checking to find the gully. Rappel 70 feet from slings around blocks down a low-angle chimney system. Hike down another short bit, and rappel from the last tree 100 feet to 3rd class slabs. Be very careful on this last rappel as the rope is just long enough; also, it is easy to accidentally stab your rope on a very sharp cactus near the tree—hooking your rope through a smaller dead tree can keep the rope out of the cactus.

From the slabs, follow the descent info for the Lower Painted Bowl (see above).

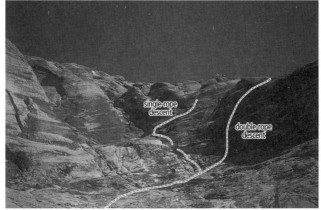

Greg Barnes

Black Orpheus 5.10a★★★★

Time to climb route: **5-6 hours**

Approach time: **1.5-2 hours**

Descent time: **3-4 hours**

Sun exposure: **mid-morning to sunset**

Height of route: **1000'**

Black Orpheus ascends a break in a huge overhung headwall via a cleanly fractured dihedral and has some of the best moderate crack climbing at Red Rocks. An initial dihedral has a few awkward sections, then a long broad slab leads up to a traverse below the headwall. The reward is the excellent upper dihedral with tons of fun climbing and a short bolt-protected crux.

History

George and Joanne Urioste accomplished the first ascent of Black Orpheus in April 1979. It was not a good time for the Uriostes. They were divorced. Though plagued by uncertainty and facing serious life decisions, they were united by a common love for climbing. A reconnaissance up the first few pitches looked very promising. The dark, south-facing rock was warm and pleasant in the still-cool spring air. The initial pitches went free and assured easy access to the spectacular crack and dihedral system on the upper part of the route.

They returned optimistically, with the intention of climbing through to the summit in one push. The climbing went well. They quickly achieved their previous high point and continued onto the upper cracks. As they reached the top of their thirteenth pitch, both daylight and crack were fading. Faced with drilling several

bolts to protect the face climbing that separated them from the summit, they had no choice but to bivouac.

Even then, their options were limited. There was no ledge big enough to stretch out on, only big enough for sitting. And, ironically, there was no spot big enough for them to sit together, so the maritally torn climbers endured the cold April night on separate ledges high above Oak Creek.

When morning finally arrived, George set out to lead the face pitch. Tired, stiff, and debilitated from the rough night, he drilled the four protection bolts on the pink face. Above this pitch the difficulties faded and the climbers were soon unroping on the summit slabs.

The name Black Orpheus derives from a 1958 movie that modernized the Greek legend of Orpheus and Eurydice to a setting during the Carnival in contemporary Rio. The movie was noted for its presentation of the Bossa Nova musical idiom, but retained the Greek myth's bittersweet story of doomed love. The relevance of the movie to the Uriostes' personal situation, combined with the darkly varnished rock, explains the selection of the route name.

– Larry DeAngelo

Strategy

Often touted as one of the easiest long routes of its grade due to a short crux, Black Orpheus lures many into epics. While the route is not particularly long, the approach and complex descent demand an early start and rapid progress. Especially important is the near impossibility of retreating out of the upper part of the route.

The second pitch has a short but awkward section of liebacking/jamming and a large nut is the best option for protection. The eighth pitch has some

Black Orpheus	Pitch	1	2	3	4	5	6	7	8	9	10	11
Free difficulty	≥5.10									●		
	5.9							●				
	5.8	●	●									
	5.7			●								
	5.6					●		●			●	●
	≤5.5				●		●					

scary face climbing off the belay, then an awkward chimney section followed by a tricky lieback. The crux, at the start of the ninth pitch, has two bolts protecting a tricky lieback/reach for an edge. However, due to the position of the bolts and the direction of the lieback, a fall could result in a short, hard pendulum into the belay ledge, and it is not possible to simply pull on a draw to bypass the crux.

If you finish the route early and have the time, consider running up Johnny Vegas or Beulah's Book, then rappelling Solar Slab Gully.

Bolts were replaced by the ASCA in 2002.

Retreat

From the first two pitches you can rappel with two ropes from bolts. From the top of the third, a long sling could be used to retreat. **Above the third pitch, retreat is not recommended and would require experienced parties.** A multi-pitch rappel while leaving gear, followed by a mandatory long traverse on 4th and 5th class slabs, followed by more gear-intensive rappels, means that retreat is basically not an option once you leave the initial dihedral.

George Urioste on Pitch 10 of Black Orpheus.

Larry DeAngelo

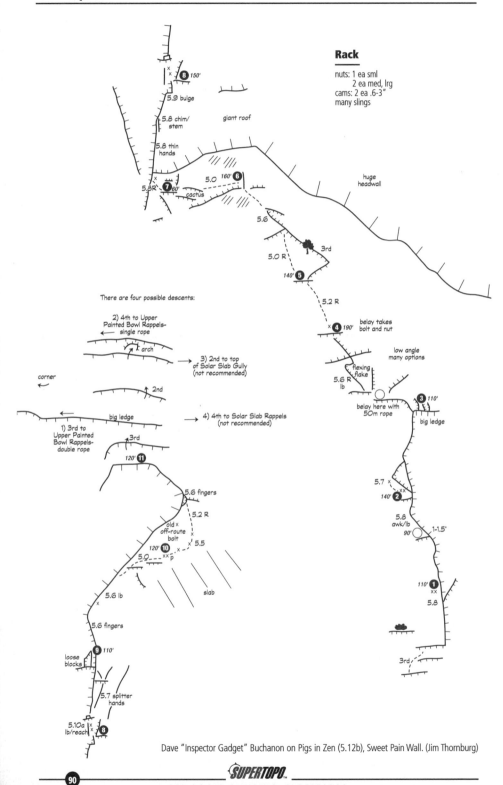

Rack

nuts: 1 ea sml
2 ea med, lrg
cams: 2 ea .6-3"
many slings

8 150'
5.9 bulge
5.8 chim/stem
giant roof
5.8 thin hands

huge headwall

5.8 R 7 60'
5.0 160' 6
cactus
5.6
5.0 R 3rd
140' 5
5.2 R

There are four possible descents:

2) 4th to Upper Painted Bowl Rappels- single rope
arch

3) 2nd to top of Solar Slab Gully (not recommended)

corner
2nd

big ledge
1) 3rd to Upper Painted Bowl Rappels- double rope

4) 4th to Solar Slab Rappels (not recommended)

x 4 190'   belay takes bolt and nut

low angle many options

flexing flake
5.6 R lb

belay here with 50m rope

3 110'
big ledge

5.7
140' 2

5.8 awk/lb
90'   1-1.5"

3rd
120' 11
5.6 fingers
5.2 R
old off-route bolt
120' 10   5.5
5.0   p
5.6 lb
slab
5.6 fingers

loose blocks 9 110'

5.7 splitter hands

5.10a lb/reach   8

110' 1
xx
5.8

3rd

Dave "Inspector Gadget" Buchanon on Pigs in Zen (5.12b), Sweet Pain Wall. (Jim Thornburg)

Solar Slab Wall

The Solar Slab Wall is one of the best larger walls at Red Rocks and it's packed with excellent moderate routes. As the name implies, it gets all day sun and is one of the few walls appropriate for mid-winter climbing. From afar it appears white and slabby and of poor quality compared to some of the dark rock walls of Red Rocks. Up close, it is large and complex with a hidden, overhung wall on its left side (the Black Orpheus Buttress), and a steep multi-pitch wall at the base of the slab. Excellent, long, and sustained routes ascend this deceptively large formation and overnight bivies and epics are common!

Approach

The approach is relatively flat and takes about 1-1.5 hours. Oak Creek Canyon is at the end of the loop road. You can also park at the old Oak Creek Campground or at an unnamed old road along the main highway and avoid the hassle of the Loop Road (an extra 20-30 minute hike in each direction).

From the Oak Creek Trailhead (there is a bathroom here), follow the old roadbed up into the canyon. Here, the road winds gently down into the streambed, with a trail departing on the right about 100 yards after the road heads downhill. Do NOT take this trail—take the next one, about 50 yards further along. Hike up the canyon, passing some large boulders via a bit of scrambling past oak trees, then head up to the base of the Solar Slab area on a variety of well-worn trails. There are two main gully systems on this wall: the major one, extending from the top of the wall to the bottom; and the left-hand one, which goes up about 500 feet before ending below the huge white slab. Solar Slab Gully is the left-hand route, yet the upper part of the right-hand one is also called "Solar Slab Gully" and is an optional (not recommended) descent for the upper routes. Head for the smaller left-hand gully—all the routes begin within 100 yards of the bottom of this gully. Beulah's Book and Johnny Vegas start to

A	Beulah's Book	E	Going Nuts
B	Johnny Vegas	F	Solar Slab
C	Solar Slab Gully	G	Horndogger Select/
D	Horndogger Select		Sundog Variation

the left of the tree-filled Solar Slab Gully; Horndogger Select starts to the right. If you reach a point where the right wall meets the wash, you've gone about 300 yards too far.

Descent

Rappel the upper routes with two ropes. Most of the lower routes either have no fixed rappel stations or lots of knobs to snag ropes, and so the recommended descent is to rappel Solar Slab Gully with a single rope, keeping the second rope coiled. This is because most of the raps are very short, and it allow you to climb back up to retrieve snagged ropes. A couple of the rap stations are in very exposed positions, and a belay is recommended for anyone uncomfortable reaching the bolts.

It is also possible to do the longer Painted Bowl descent to get off these routes, and it is the only way to descend the upper tier routes with a single rope. See the descent description in the Black Orpheus descent section.

Once at the base, reverse the approach to the car. With rappels, it takes most people 3-4 hours to descend from the top of the upper tier; from the top of the first tier routes, it takes about 2 hours.

Beulah's Book 5.9★★★★

Time to climb route: **1-2 hours**

Approach time: **1 hour**

Descent time: **1-2 hours**

Sun exposure: **all day**

Height of route: **1400'**

Intimidating looking chimneys in a corner, Beulah's Book doesn't usually get the credit it deserves. It is one of the finest three-pitch routes of its grade in Red Rocks, and with a wild new arête variation, requires little in the way of chimney skills. The striking upper part of the book above the chimneys has outstanding climbing.

FA: Randal Grandstaff, Dave Anderson, 1979.

Strategy

While not as popular as Johnny Vegas or Solar Slab Gully, Beulah's Book still gets lines and so an early start is recommended, especially if you do plan to continue higher. No wide protection is needed for the climb if you use the arête variation on the second pitch; a single 4-inch piece is all that is needed to supplement the rack for the original route.

The first pitch has a few tricky moves off the ground, but then has sweet climbing up a face/arête just left of a deep chimney. The second pitch has a bombay chimney crux protected by a bolt and a 4-inch cam, or a stellar new arête variation that is protected by thin nuts, a medium cam, and three bolts. The top of the pitch is a long 5.9 lieback section with good rests; long slings on the protection at the bottom of the pitch are recommended to reduce rope drag.

The third pitch is substantially runout on low-angle knobs and edges, and thin nuts and cams can be found with some searching.

Retreat

You can rap from any pitch except the third with two ropes, but it's easy to traverse to the upper anchor of Johnny Vegas or to descend Solar Slab Gully.

Stephen Cherry in the Pitch 2 chimney of Beulah's Book.

Larry DeAngelo

Beulah's Book		Pitch 1	2	3
Free difficulty	≥5.10			
	5.9		●	
	5.8	●		
	5.7			
	5.6			●
	≤5.5			

Johnny Vegas 5.6 R★★★★★

Time to climb route: **1-2 hours**	
Approach time: **1 hour**	
Descent time: **1-2 hours**	
Sun exposure: **all day**	
Height of route: **1400'**	

Solar Slab Gully 5.3★★★

Time to climb route: **1-2 hours**	
Approach time: **1 hour**	
Descent time: **1-2 hours**	
Sun exposure: **all day**	
Height of route: **1400'**	

Johnny Vegas is the most recent of the three variations people use to approach Solar Slab above. It was somehow overlooked for years despite its excellent moderate climbing. On its own it is a fun climb on steep juggy rock, and in combination with Solar Slab and/or Going Nuts, is one of the longest and best 5.6 routes anywhere.

FA: Harrison Shull, Tom Cecil, Dave Cox, Todd Hewitt, 11/94.

Strategy

Lines are common on this climb, and if you want to climb all of Solar Slab and descend before dark, a very early start is recommended. The Loop Road opens at 6 a.m.—the slightly longer hike from Highway 159 at the old Oak Creek Campground is the best way to beat the crowds.

Most of the climbing is juggy face, but some loose or hollow rock is found here and there, and care should be used to avoid breaking holds. The main challenge is a slabby runout off the belay on the third pitch. Knobs can be tied off for protection, and there are good edges to use, but the leader should be confident on such climbing. A thin 5.9 corner with a bolt-protected face is an alternate option for this section.

Retreat

You can rap from any pitch with two ropes.

Solar Slab Gully is one of the easiest multi-pitch climbs at Red Rocks. With abundant bolted anchors, short pitches, and with an easy approach, it is extremely popular. However, it is all chimney and gully climbing and even with a low rating, many climbers are not experienced at such climbing. It is a fine mountaineering and canyoneering adventure, but is not up to the quality and exposure of most moderate Red Rocks climbs.

FA: Unknown.

Strategy

Start early, and be prepared for much wide crack climbing and stemming. Protection is abundant but often awkward to place.

The crux for most people is finding the easiest way up; the first pitch looks improbable as it face climbs up past a black offwidth. Follow the topo closely. Only a single 50m rope is needed for this climb, but if you continue up Solar Slab, two will be required for rappelling the route (the standard descent).

The route is a waterfall at the crux, so if a storm hits, get out quick. If you start late, beware of climbers descending the gully. It's possible to bivy on top of the route.

Retreat

Rap from any pitch with one 50m rope. Longer rappels can lead to rope snags.

Johnny Vegas		Pitch 1	2	3	4
Free difficulty	≥5.10				
	5.9			●	
	5.8			●	
	5.7			●	
	5.6	●	●	●	
	≤5.5				●

Solar Slab Gully		Pitch 1	2	3	4
Free difficulty	≥5.5				
	5.4				
	5.3				●
	5.2				
	5.1	●		●	
	4th		●		

A. Beulah's Book 5.9★★★★ nuts: 1 set; cams: 2 ea .6-1.5", 1 ea 2-3", 1 ea 4"

B. Johnny Vegas 5.6 R★★★★★ nuts: 1 set; cams: 2 ea .6-2", 1 ea 3"; many slings

C. Solar Slab Gully 5.3★★★ nuts: 1 set; cams: 1 ea .6-1", 2 ea 1.25-3", 1 ea 4"; many slings

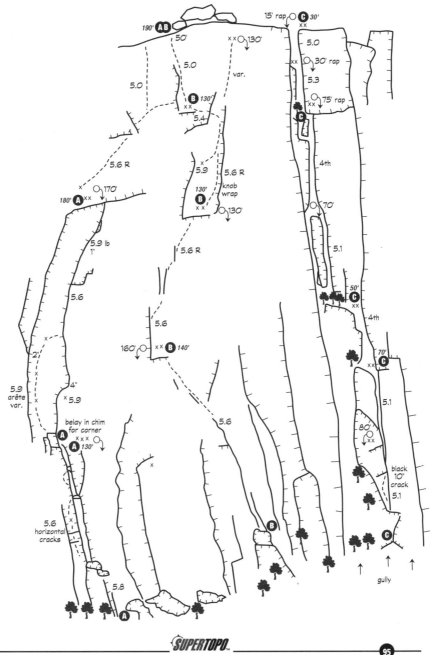

Solar Slab 5.6★★★★★

Time to climb route: **4-6 hours**

Approach time: **3-4 hours**

Descent time: **3-4 hours**

Sun exposure: **all day**

Height of route: **1500'**

Solar Slab is one of the best moderate climbs in the U.S. In combination with routes below, it offers 1,500 feet of climbing, with sunny and warm weather even in winter. It follows the obvious system of cracks and flakes up the middle of the huge white slab, and the climbing is predominantly face climbing with finger and hand cracks for protection.

FA: Joe Herbst, Tom Kaufmann, Larry Hamilton, 1/75.

History

This was truly the A-team of early Red Rocks climbing. Joe Herbst, with either Larry or Tom as his partner, was responsible for the ascents of the Big three walls of Red Rocks (Velvet Wall, Rainbow Wall, and Aeolian Wall). The dramatically blank appearance of the Solar Slab hides the fact that the climbing is surprisingly easy. The first ascent of the 1,500-foot wall took this well-polished party a mere 6 hours. They made it back to the base with sunshine to spare on a short January day.

Later that spring, the well-traveled Fred Beckey showed up in Las Vegas in his endless quest for new routes. Spying this piece of rock, he attacked it as a big wall project, and spent two days completing an early repeat of the route. Unaware that it had seen a prior ascent, he submitted the climb to the *American Alpine Journal* with the name "Solar Plexus."

– Larry DeAngelo

Solar Slab		Pitch 1	2	3	4	5	6	7
Free difficulty	≥5.10							
	5.9							
	5.8							
	5.7							
	5.6	●	●	●	●			
	≤5.5					●	●	●

Strategy

The biggest problem with a classic 5.6 is, not surprisingly, the crowds. Start early, and even then there is usually a "race" up the first routes to the base of Solar Slab. Luckily, the outstanding route Going Nuts, also 5.6, is a great alternative to the first two pitches of Solar Slab (see below). Still, a traffic jam on the upper pitches of Solar Slab is often unavoidable.

The first pitch is the psychological crux for most, since the original route ascends an unprotected face for half a pitch straight up to the beautiful crack. You can climb to the right with protection, but this requires breaking the pitch in two. At the start of the third pitch is a short traverse protected by thin nuts in plates, followed by a shallow fingercrack. The start of the fourth pitch also has a traverse, this time followed by a lieback section with intermittent protection.

In warm weather the climb is way too hot, but in colder weather it is usually perfect.

Retreat

Rappel the route with two ropes from any pitch. See the topo for rappel options.

A. Going Nuts   5.6★★★★

FA: Unknown

Beautiful climbing on steep, juggy black rock, Going Nuts would easily be the best 5.6 route at most climbing areas in the world. Ascending the midst of the large face under the arch left of Solar Slab, it follows thin crack systems and a juggy face on plates, passing the left end of the arch on the second pitch. The plates at the first pitch belay and on the second pitch are beautiful and offer unique climbing. The top of the second pitch is a large bushy ledge, and it's a short walk to the right to join Solar Slab's second pitch belay. There is some loose rock on this route, especially on the second pitch after the arch is passed. It would be possible to retreat from the first pitch belay by leaving a few large nuts; two ropes would be required.

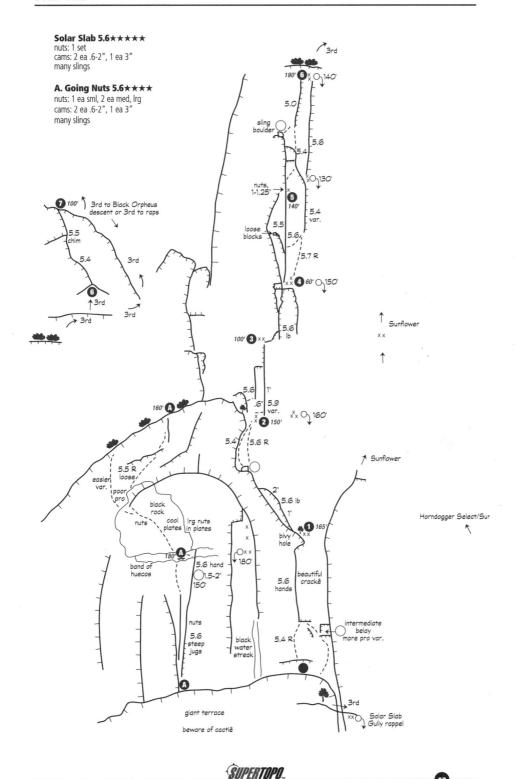

Solar Slab 5.6★★★★★
nuts: 1 set
cams: 2 ea .6-2", 1 ea 3"
many slings

A. Going Nuts 5.6★★★★
nuts: 1 ea sml, 2 ea med, lrg
cams: 2 ea .6-2", 1 ea 3"
many slings

3rd

190' ⑥ 140'

5.0

sling boulder

5.6

5.4

130'

⑦ 100'   3rd to Black Orpheus descent or 3rd to raps

nuts, 1-1.25"

⑤ 140'

5.5 chim

5.4 var.

5.4

3rd

loose blocks

5.5

5.6

⑥

3rd

5.7 R

3rd

3rd

⑤ 60' 150'

5.6 lb

100' ③

Sunflower

5.6   1"

.6"   5.9 var.

160' Ⓐ

② 150'   160'

5.4   5.6 R

Sunflower

5.5 R loose

easier var.

poor pro

2"

5.6 lb

black rock

1"

cool plates

lrg nuts in plates

① 165'

nuts

bivy hole

Horndogger Select/Sur

180' Ⓐ

5.6 hand

180'

beautiful crackê

band of huecos

1.5-2" 150'

5.6 hands

nuts

5.6 steep jugs

black water streak

5.4 R

intermediate belay more pro var.

Ⓐ

3rd

giant terrace

beware of cactiê

Solar Slab Gully rappel

Horndogger Select to Sundog 5.10a★★★

Time to climb route: **5-7 hours**	
Approach time: **1 hour**	
Descent time: **2-3 hours**	
Sun exposure: **all day**	
Height of route: **1500'**	

Horndogger Select and the Sundog variation to the top of Horndogger Select offer excellent climbing on somewhat delicate and less traveled rock. The first three pitches can be used to access the huge ledge at the base of Solar Slab, and likewise, Solar Slab Gully, Johnny Vegas, or Beulah's Book can be used to access the upper part of Horndogger Select and Sundog. Long and varied, with everything from steep face and crack to slab and thin edging, Horndogger Select to Sundog is a fun outing for climbers experienced at the grade, and a great choice for a longer mid-winter route on fully south-facing rock.

FA: David Pollari, Shawn Pereto, Brian Kaye 2/93.
FA of Sundog finish: Ed Prochaska, Joanne Urioste.

Strategy

The first section of Horndogger Select (the first three pitches to the giant ledge) is steep climbing on large and often suspect holds. With very little traffic, some tricky routefinding, and no fixed anchors, this first section is a welcome relief from the almost constant crowds on its neighbors. Many holds on these first three pitches are large, but some are very thin as well, and care should be exercised to avoid breaking holds.

Horndogger Select to Sundog

Solar Slab Gully

Greg Barnes

The upper section of Horndogger Select originally finished high on the route with a traverse out left below a roof on loose rock. A new route/variation, Sundog, heads straight through the roof on positive holds past a tightly bolted 5.10a section, then continues straight up the wall beyond. With a few sections of 5.7 runout climbing, including a particularly dangerous one on large loose horns straight off the belay, it is a somewhat serious outing. Luckily, you rappel the route with two ropes anyway, so if things start looking too difficult, retreat is easy.

Retreat

Rap the upper section with two ropes from bolted belays. Rap Solar Slab Gully to descend from the first three pitches. If you get hit by a rainstorm, don't descend the gully since it is a waterfall in several spots; instead, rappel Johnny Vegas (gear may need to be left to gain the uppermost bolts).

Horndogger Select	Pitch	1	2	3	4	5	6	7	8
Free difficulty	≥5.10					•			
	5.9								•
	5.8	•	•	•			•		
	5.7					•			
	5.6								
	≤5.5			•					

Rack

nuts: 2 ea sml, med
     1 ea lrg
cams: 2 ea .6-3"
(for last pitch: either cams: 1 ea 4-6", or 1 ea .2-.33")
Lowe Balls; screamers advised on tiny gear if taking right finish.)

x x **8** 130'

5.9+ R

.2'
.3'   licheny
     1' face

sml Lowe Balls
+ OO TCU

4-6'
5.9

5.9 awk.

x x **7** 115'   Sundog finish

x

x 5.10a slabby face
x 5.9 overhang

Horndogger
finish

loose blocks
runout

5.7 R
scary horns

x x **6** 140'
black rock

don't clip sling
on horns or place
pro behind them❓

p (2 nuts)

x
5.7 R
x
5.8
x
x

180' **5** x x

5.7
nuts   wide
          crack

100' ◯ 2-3.5"

x
5.6 R
x

black

x
4   3rd

upper
Horndogger
and Sundog   ↑

4 xx" 3rd

runout
face var.

3rd

x x

140' **3**

5.8
slab

black
rock

Solar
Slab ↑
Gully

5.7
3'   belay takes
2 **2** 160' 2-3'   giant ledge
move belay
to base of crack

steep
5.8
fingers

large, black
huecos in
groove

5.6

1 150' belay takes
1.25-1.5" cams
and nuts

1'
5.8

opt. belay
.75-2" ◯   5.8

↗ The Friar

5.7

belay
cave

Pine Creek Canyon
Juniper Canyon

A large, varied canyon with a fairly short approach hike, Pine Creek is the second-to-last stop on the Loop Road and has a good sized paved parking lot with bathrooms. Brass Wall and Cat in the Hat are south-facing and among the warmest climbing spots covered in this guide, while Dark Shadows is cold and shady.

Basically a spur off of Pine Creek, Juniper Canyon is accessed from either Pine Creek or the Loop Road trailhead for Oak Creek. Crimson Chrysalis, located in Juniper Canyon, gets morning sun and is often perfect temperature through most of spring and fall, but is usually too cold in winter and cold spells.

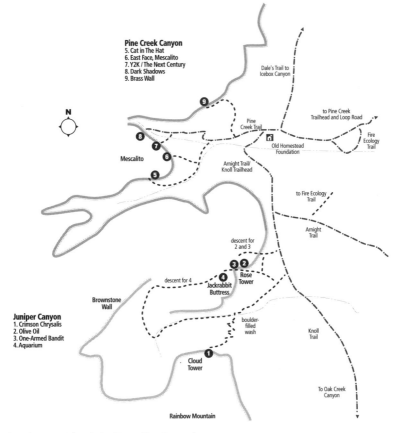

John Helman on Pitch 5 of Cloud Tower. (Greg Epperson)

Cloud Tower

Regardless of where you are on the main Loop Road, the striking red summit of Cloud Tower calls out to be climbed. Located at the mouth of Juniper Canyon, the tower stands proudly above a steep slope, adding prominence and exposure. Cloud Tower is renowned for sustained and steep moves on excellent rock. It is also one of the few formations with a real summit, one that is small enough to feel exposed but large enough so that you can comfortably hang out.

Approach

This approach is about 1.5 miles long and gains about 1,000 feet in elevation.

From Pine Creek Trailhead, hike on the main trail down the hill and up Pine Creek. Go past the Fire Ecology Trail (two entrances, it is a short loop), past an unnamed trail on the left, to the main Arnight/Knoll Trail (just past the prominent concrete foundation of the old homestead; about 15-20 minutes from the car). Cross the creek, go right for 150 feet, then follow the nicely graded trail left and up the far bank. Hike on the trail for about 10 minutes, then take the right trail heading toward Cloud Tower. The first prominent trail on the right is the approach to Rose

Sarah Felchlin

Sarah Felchlin

Tower and the Northeast Face of Jackrabbit Buttress (the descent trail from Rose Tower intersects earlier, but it is hard to see from the main trail). To continue on to Crimson Chrysalis, Geronimo, or anything up the main Juniper Canyon (Brownstone Wall, Rainbow Wall), stay on the left trail. After another few hundred yards, a trail heads left across the rocky wash toward Cloud Tower (Crimson etc), while the main Juniper Canyon trail heads up the canyon. From here, many steep trails switchback up the ramp. Head toward the upper right hand corner of the ramp to approach the base of Crimson Chrysalis. The route starts up an obvious right-facing corner and crack.

An alternate approach starts from the junction of Highway 159 and the exit gate of the Loop Road. Reverse the Loop Road on foot to the Oak Creek Trailhead. Turn right on the Arnight Trail that leads to the Knoll Trail. This adds another 2 miles to the approach, but gives a head start on climbers who use the Loop Road, which doesn't open until 6 a.m.

Descent

Rappel the route with two 50m or 60m ropes. Be aware that other climbers are surely below. The cracks tend to eat ropes so pull ropes to the right and away from the crack. Reverse the approach trail back to the car.

Crimson Chrysalis 5.8★★★★★

Time to climb route: **5-8 hours**

Approach time: **1-1.5 hours**

Descent time: **1-1.5 hours**

Sun exposure: **early morning**

Height of route: **1000'**

Crimson Chrysalis is the best 5.8 in Red Rocks. Both the rock quality and climbing remain consistently awesome from the first pitch to the last. It is predominantly a face climb that avoids wide cracks via bolt-protected steep and fun edges. The wall looks too steep for 5.8, but good holds always show up where needed. Cracks are primarily used just for protection but occasionally mandatory jams appear. The difficulties are sustained and sometimes gear is sparse, making the route suitable only for confident 5.8 leaders.

History

The first ascent was completed with four fixed ropes by George and Joanne Urioste in October 1979. The name stems from the red coloration of the rock and physical resemblance of the pillar to a huge butterfly's cocoon. George recalls the first ascent as a fairly bold undertaking. There were fewer bolts placed than were mentioned in the red book. Some leads were runout enough that one could be seriously hurt in a fall. George says they worked pretty hard to avoid bolting by tying off small horns and flakes, and placing nuts in shallow surface features.

Shortly after the fixed ropes were pulled, Joanne and Randal Grandstaff returned and did the first continuous ascent. In the following months the route was repeated by several other parties, and some felt that more bolts were needed. George and Joanne were of the opinion that the route was "too beautiful not to share," so they went back and added a few protection bolts, and beefed up the belays. The route was thus brought up to the state reported in the original 1984 guidebook. The subsequent popularity of the route with ordinary climbers as well as guided parties has led to the addition of even more bolts. If the route has lost a bit of the commitment element, it has become a highly accessible and magnificent climb.

One irony of their ascent became evident to George as they rappelled from the summit of the tower. On their last pitch, they had climbed through a small overhang then veered right. The rightward traverse was protected by a few bolts and gained the top near the corner of the wall. As they rappelled, George spotted a line of holds leading straight up from the overhang. "THAT'S where the route should have gone!" he thought. Unfortunately, the bolts were already in, and the indirect line has been the standard ever since.

– Larry DeAngelo

Strategy

Crowds are almost certain and even a pre-dawn start does not guarantee that you will be first in line. Avoid this climb on weekends. Fast climbers can climb in the afternoon after the morning rush but climbers will be rapping over them.

This north-facing route is shaded, making it perfect for warm fall or spring days. During most of the year bring a wind shell and warm gloves. Night descents are common, so bring a headlamp, extra batteries, and a warm jacket.

Crimson Chrysalis	Pitch	1	2	3	4	5	6	7	8	9
Free difficulty	≥5.10									
	5.9									
	5.8	●	●	●	●	●				●
	5.7							●	●	
	5.6						●			
	≤5.5									

Aside from a short, distinct crux on Pitch 5, the climbing is remarkably sustained at 5.8. If anything, the climbing is psychologically easier up high as you adapt to the exposure and sometimes-hollow holds. Uncomfortable hanging belays are the norm so wear comfortable shoes and harness. While there is usually a bolt or natural gear placement right where you want it, be ready for the occasional short runout on easier terrain.

At the base, be sure to hang your backpack off the ground and out of the reach of hungry varmints.

Retreat

Rappel from any pitch with two ropes.

Ben Snead on the Pitch 4 awesome edges of Crimson Chrysalis.

Sarah Felchlin

Rack

nuts: 1 set
cams: 1 ea .6-3"
extra 1-4" (optional)
8 quickdraws
many slings
50m or 60m rappel rope

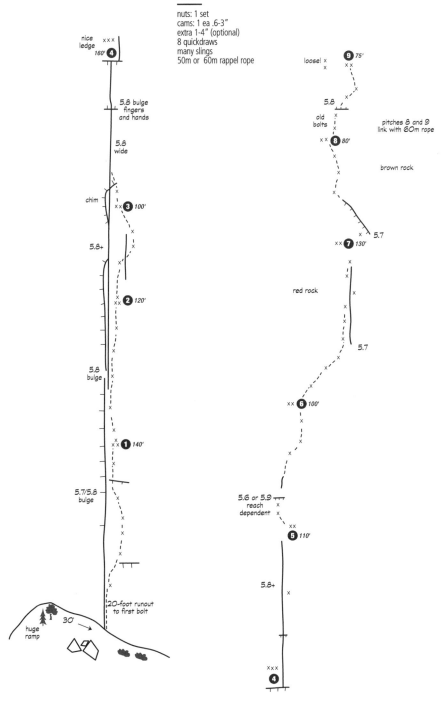

nice
ledge   x x x
        160' ❹

5.8 bulge
fingers
and hands

5.8
wide

chim   x
       x x ❸ 100'

5.8+   x
        x

        x
       x x ❷ 120'
        x

        x

5.8
bulge   x

        x
       x x ❶ 140'
        x

5.7/5.8   x
bulge
           x

           x

           x

           x
20-foot runout
to first bolt

huge   30' →
ramp

loose! x   x x ❾ 75'
          x

          x
5.8   x

old   x
bolts   x
       x x ❽ 80'

pitches 8 and 9
link with 60m rope

brown rock

                    x
                   x x ❼ 130'   5.7
                        x
red rock   x
                        x   x

                        x
                        x   5.7
                        x
                       x

                      x
                     x
                x x ❻ 100'
                x
                x

5.6 or 5.9 ⊤⊤⊤
reach   x
dependent   x
          x x
          ❺ 110'

5.8+   x

       x x x
       ❹

Jackrabbit Buttress, South Face

Greg Barnes

A "small" formation opposite of Crimson Chrysalis in Juniper Canyon, the South Face of Jackrabbit Buttress is easily overlooked. This may explain why the stellar 5.6 route Geronimo was not climbed until 1992. With full sun most of the day and a reasonably short approach, this is an excellent choice for cooler weather.

Approach

From Pine Creek Trailhead, hike on the main trail down the hill and up the main trail up Pine Creek. Go past the Fire Ecology Trail (two entrances, it is a short loop), past an unnamed trail on the left, to the main Arnight/Knoll Trail (just past the prominent concrete foundation of the old homestead—about 15-20 minutes from the car). Cross the creek, go right for 150 feet, then follow the nicely graded trail left and up the far bank. Hike on the trail for about 10 minutes, then take the right trail heading toward Cloud Tower. The first prominent trail on the right is the approach to Rose Tower and the Northeast Face of Jackrabbit Buttress (the descent trail from Rose Tower intersects earlier, but it is hard to see from the main trail). To continue on to Crimson Chrysalis, Geronimo, or anything up the main Juniper Canyon (Brownstone Wall, Rainbow Wall), stay on the left trail. After another few hundred yards, a trail heads left across the rocky wash toward Cloud Tower (Crimson Chrysalis, etc.), while the main Juniper Canyon trail heads up the canyon. At the mouth of the canyon, a small use trail heads up and right—this is the approach for Geronimo.

Descent

Rap from the top with two ropes. Once at the big ledge after the first rap, stow one rope and rappel four more times with a single rope, using care to keep the rope out of the cracks. Rope snags are common, and if needed, you can use the second rope to re-lead and retrieve the rope. The last three raps are from trees or slung chockstones, and extra long webbing may be needed to replace old webbing.

Geronimo 5.6★★★★

Time to climb route: **2-3 hours**

Approach time: **1-1.5 hours**

Descent time: **2 hours**

Sun exposure: **morning to afternoon**

Height of route: **500'**

Geronimo is one of the best routes of the grade in Red Rocks. It has steep, juggy climbing up successive tiers of rock. With face, crack, stemming, and arête climbing, often with incut edges and jugs, Geronimo is a joy to climb. Huge belay ledges and a wild finish up an exposed arête just add to the appeal. The rap route stays right of the climb, reducing tangles. Despite its quality, it is a relatively new climb, and there are many large holds which are somewhat thin and delicate, especially on the first pitch.

FA: Bill Cramer, Michelle Cramer, 5/92.

Strategy

Lines are fairly common at Geronimo, but as the rap route is separate from the climb, and the belay ledges are huge (except the third), other parties are not much of a headache. It is common to climb Geronimo in combination with another route, such as Olive Oil or Crimson Chrysalis. Two 50m ropes are required for the descent, but a 60m rope is an advantage for the long pitches.

Retreat

Retreat by rappelling the rap route (see topo). It is easy to gain the rap anchors from the second and fourth belays, but at the first and third belays, gear would need to be left to rappel.

Rack

nuts: 1 set
cams: 1 ea .6, 3", 2 ea .75-2"
two ropes

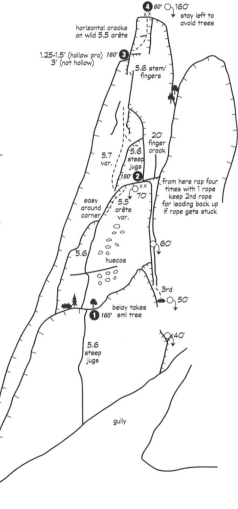

Geronimo	Pitch			
	1	2	3	4
Free difficulty ≥5.10				
5.9				
5.8				
5.7				
5.6	●	●	●	
≤5.5				●

Rose Tower

From a distance, Rose Tower and its neighbor, Jackrabbit Buttress, look like little more than bumps compared to the towering Rainbow Wall and Brownstone Wall. Up close however, they are not small at all, offering excellent routes from four to eight pitches. Rose Tower is hidden from sight along the normal hiking approach (from Pine Creek trailhead), but once in sight the beautiful rose-colored rock at the top makes its naming obvious. The rock quality is not always great, but the classic Olive Oil is super solid.

Approach

From Pine Creek trailhead, hike on the main trail down the hill and up the main trail up Pine Creek. Go past the Fire Ecology Trail (two entrances, it is a short loop), past an unnamed trail on the left, to the main Arnight/Knoll Trail (just past the prominent concrete foundation of the old homestead—about 15-20 minutes from the car). Cross the creek, go right for 150 feet, then follow the nicely graded trail left and up the far bank. Hike on the trail for about 10 minutes, then take the right trail heading towards Cloud Tower. The first prominent trail on the right is the approach to Rose Tower and the Northeast Face of Jackrabbit Buttress (the descent trail from Rose Tower intersects earlier, but it is hard to see from the main trail). To continue on to Crimson Chrysalis, Geronimo, or anything up the main Juniper Canyon (Brownstone Wall, Rainbow Wall), stay on the left trail.

Descent

From the top of Olive Oil (also the top of One-Armed Bandit), scramble up and left to the top of the formation, and hike back along the ridge top then down the gully. There is a 10-foot 4th class downclimb just before you reach the gully—use care here, and the first down can spot partner(s).

Olive Oil 5.7 R★★★★★

Time to climb route:	**2-3 hours**
Approach time:	**1 hour**
Descent time:	**1.5 hours**
Sun exposure:	**afternoon**
Height of route:	**550'**

Olive Oil is one of the best Red Rocks moderates with its excellent, varied climbing on great rock. The long, awesome crack on the second and third pitches, some routefinding on easier terrain, and a final huge stemming dihedral all add up to a great day. With some runout sections at 5.7, it is not a good climb to break into that grade.

FA: George and Joanne Urioste, John Williamson, 2/78. Portions may have been climbed by Joe Herbst & Larry Hamilton, 1/76, during FA of Rose Tower.

History

John Williamson was one of Red Rocks' original pioneers, but he had been out of Las Vegas since the early 1970s. During a visit in 1978 he teamed up with George and Joanne Urioste for several routes. Olive Oil is most notable to today's climbers for its clean rock and moderate difficulties. In his younger days, John would often acquire climbing partners by introducing some innocent friend to the sport. Frequently they were overwhelmed by his drive and enthusiasm, so John was especially happy to meet the Uriostes, who were at least as overboard as he was.

John recalls that after Olive Oil they were driving back to town in the gathering twilight. As they proceeded along what was then a deserted stretch of West Charleston Boulevard, George ran over a jackrabbit.

He brought the car to an immediate stop, backed up, jumped out and retrieved the rabbit. He took it home and cooked it (in curry sauce John recalls 25 years later!). John says, "I don't remember that Joanne and I ate a whole lot of it."

John probably doesn't realize how lucky he was. George says, "I always wanted to try everything. The worst we ever had was a coyote. That wasn't good at all. One time we found a bobcat that someone hit and that was the best."

– *Larry DeAngelo*

Strategy

Immensely popular, it is difficult to get to Olive Oil without others ahead of you. Start at the gate the moment the Loop Road is open, have your packs ready, and head straight for the climb. Alternatively, wait until late in the day—it is common to climb Olive Oil after first doing another nearby route such as Crimson Chrysalis or Geronimo (which both have the same crowding issues).

The first pitch is the serious section, with 5.7 face climbing without great protection to the left of a polished chimney. The fourth pitch goes up a crack system, then heads to the right to gain the top of a pillar —this unlikely traverse to the right is where people get off-route. The final dihedral is runout on easy terrain down low, then better protected (but not great protection) through a steep chimney section.

Retreat

Retreat with two ropes from bolted belays and/or natural protection. Note that all the bolted belays on this climb were added by unknown parties around 2002, and may be chopped at any time because they are not original and reduce the commitment factor on this classic traditional route.

Olive Oil		Pitch 1	2	3	4	5	6
Free difficulty	≥5.10						
	5.9						
	5.8						
	5.7	●	●	●		●	
	5.6				●		
	≤5.5						●

One-Armed Bandit 5.7 R★★

Time to climb route: **2-3 hours**

Approach time: **1 hour**

Descent time: **1.5 hours**

Sun exposure: **afternoon**

Height of route: **500'**

Loose and runout, One-Armed Bandit is typical of much of the less-than-classic routes at Red Rocks. Of course, this also gives you the flavor of many of the classic routes before lots of traffic cleaned them up. Most of the climbing on One-Armed Bandit is fun and well protected, but a few sections of loose and runout climbing make this route a serious undertaking, definitely not suitable for those with little experience on such routes.

FA: Larry Hamilton, Tom Kaufman, 3/76.

History

In March of 1976, Tom Kaufman was climbing with Joe Herbst at the Sheep Skull Crag. He was leading the Black Glass Corner when he fell. Tom says, "It was an awkward fall. I came flying out of the crack, except my foot kind of stuck. I tried to catch the rope, but I ended up upside down with a dislocated shoulder." He managed to pop it back in, but it was extremely sore. This slowed him down a little, but, after all, he was in Red Rocks to climb. Two days later, he was back on the rock. Joe was busy that day, but another Red Rocks pioneer was also in town. So Tom teamed up with Larry Hamilton of Rainbow and Aeolian Wall fame.

They needed to find a route that would not be too stressful on Tom's injured shoulder. Larry was familiar with the Rose Tower area because, a few months before, he had joined Joe for a climb that started to the right of the current Olive Oil line. Their route was the first on the formation and called simply "the Rose Tower." It was pleasant and moderate, so Larry thought they could pick out another reasonable line in the same area. They started climbing uphill and to left of the old route, and stayed left to maintain an independent line. Larry did all the leading, since Tom's shoulder made it impossible for him to pull up with that arm. Their day turned out to be perfect. The weather was sunny. The climbing was good, with a few runouts but no real crux. It was just what they were looking for. Larry says, "Tom suggested the name One-Armed Bandit, and I immediately liked this not just as a reference to him, but because the formation as a whole looked a little like a slot machine in profile."

– Larry DeAngelo

Strategy

While Olive Oil has crowds, there is little chance of seeing anyone on One-Armed Bandit, unless they are retreating from Olive Oil, or off-route high on Olive Oil.

Several belays on One-Armed Bandit do not take any good protection, and while experienced climbers used to body belays will be completely comfortable due to good ledges and spots to wedge your body into, those used to setting a bomber anchor and hanging from it may be in for a rude surprise. Very large protection may allow good anchors to be set in at least one location (the base of the chimney).

Retreat

If a retreat is needed, there are a few spots without any reasonable protection available for a retreat, even including cams. There are no fixed anchors, yet at most points good anchors could be constructed, especially with long slings/cordalettes around blocks and horns.

One-Armed Bandit		Pitch 1	2	3	4	5
Free difficulty	≥5.10					
	5.9					
	5.8					
	5.7	●	●	●	●	●
	5.6					
	≤5.5					

A. Olive Oil 5.7 R★★★★★
nuts: 1 set
cams: 1 ea .6-.75", 3", 2 ea 1-2"

B. One-Armed Bandit 5.7 R★★
nuts: 1 set
cams: 1 ea .5-3", optional 4-7"
many slings

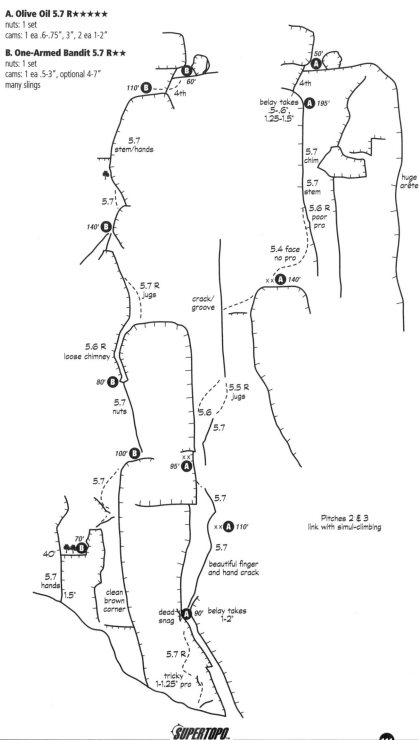

Pitches 2 & 3
link with simul-climbing

Jackrabbit Buttress, Northeast Face

Greg Barnes

The Northeast Face of Jackrabbit Buttress is the beautiful black wall opposite of Olive Oil. Despite the excellent rock, multiple obvious crack systems, and the presence of at least six routes with bolted rappel anchors, there is no previously published information or notes in the new route book at Desert Rock Sports. The approach can involve tedious bushwacking, and there are no trails once past Olive Oil.

Approach

To reach Aquarium, approach as for Olive Oil (see page 108). Once at Olive Oil, go across the 100-foot-wide gully from the base, and up through a 3rd class chimney under a huge boulder. Continue up hugging the wall opposite Olive Oil, then head around left on the first ledge (wide and bushy, some bushwacking). Contour on this ledge system, then head down a bit to the only bush-free section of the wall. Rope up here and climb a short 5.5 pitch, with bushwacking at the top (watch for cactus). This gains the wide, clean ledge at the base of the black wall. The approach is about 15 minutes from the start of Olive Oil.

Descent

Rappel 30 feet off an overhang from fixed slings/nut/tricam, then scramble about 1/4 mile along the 3rd class ridge, heading for the right end of the Brownstone Wall. Once at the wall, head down left on trails, then follow cairns down into the main canyon. Follow the canyon out to the mouth, then well-worn trails back to either Pine Creek or Oak Creek trailheads. Total descent time is about 2 hours back to the car.

Dan McQuade on the splitter Pitch 6 of Cloud Tower. (Greg Epperson)

Aquarium 5.9 R★★★

Time to climb route: **4-6 hours**

Approach time: **1 hour**

Descent time: **2 hours**

Sun exposure: **early morning**

Height of route: **1000'**

Aquarium has seen little traffic, yet is an outstanding adventure for solid climbers on rock with delicate holds. Sections of perfect black rock with solid pro are interspersed with runouts, friable rock, and routefinding difficulties. Many variations and entirely separate routes are possible on this rarely climbed piece of rock, which would in most climbing areas in the world be the most sought after wall in the area—yet in Red Rocks, it has remained undocumented and may see one ascent every few years.

Strategy

Aquarium has probably seen less than five ascents (and likely only one ascent as it is documented in SuperTopo). A huge cam may protect the crux section which is unfortunately close to the belay on thin and delicate holds. Be forewarned that this is a serious undertaking for those not familiar with friable holds. Some loose rock is found in various spots, yet the route generally traverses back and forth enough to keep the belayer out of harm's way. A 60m rope is mandatory.

Retreat

Retreat would require leaving pro. As is typical of much of Red Rocks routes, large nuts, hexes, and slings around horns would be sufficient at most points.

		Pitch							
Aquarium		1	2	3	4	5	6	7	8
Free difficulty	≥5.10								
	5.9	●	●						
	5.8				●				
	5.7			●			●	●	
	5.6				●				●
	≤5.5								

Rack

nuts: 1 set
cams: 1 ea .4-.75"
     2 ea 1-3"
     1 ea 4"
optional: 7" at crux, extra 1.5-2"

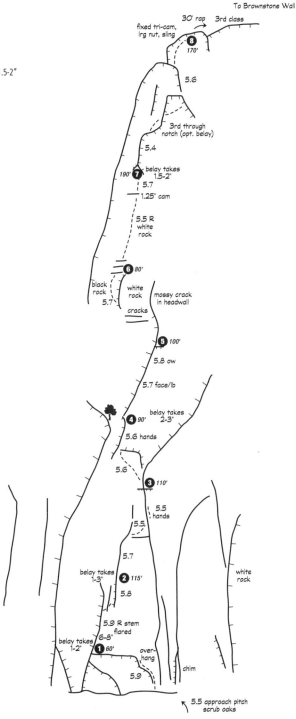

To Brownstone Wall

fixed tri-cam,   30' rap   3rd class
lrg nut, sling

8 170'

5.6

3rd through
notch (opt. belay)

5.4

190' **7**   belay takes
     1.5-2"
5.7

1.25" cam

5.5 R
white
rock

6 80'

black   white
rock   rock   mossy crack
5.7   in headwall
cracks

5 100'

5.8 ow

5.7 face/lb

4 90'   belay takes
      2-3"
5.6 hands

5.6

3 110'

5.5
hands

5.5

5.7

belay takes   **2** 115'   white
1-3"   rock
5.8

5.9 R stem
      flared
belay takes   6-8"
1-2"   **1** 60'
        over-
        hang   chim
5.9

5.5 approach pitch
scrub oaks

Mescalito

Tiny from afar, Mescalito is a natural pyramid of rock splitting Pine Creek Canyon. The north side is dark and forbidding—the base lush with huge trees and a year-round stream with small waterfalls. The south side is lower angle, with gullies, dihedrals, and a dry and hot microclimate.

Sarah Felchlin

1	Cat in the Hat	4	Next Century
2	Pine Nuts	5	Dark Shadows
3	Y2K		

Mescalito is dwarfed by the surrounding peaks, yet offers routes up to almost 1,000 feet in length. The upper sections tend to be loose however, and the most popular routes rise to only about half of the height of the wall. With a relatively simple and quick approach, and some of the best easier climbs in Red Rocks, Mescalito is often the first stop for those visiting the longer routes of Red Rocks.

Approach

The Pine Creek parking lot is most of the way around the loop road. Popular with both climbers and hikers, the rush is on as soon as the gate opens and the lot can fill early. The trail is large, well-worn, and easy to follow until almost at Mescalito, where one branch dives down left into the creek bed (almost always completely dry).

Mescalito South, Cat in the Hat

To get to Cat in the Hat, follow the left branch of the creek past a series of steep dihedrals. Stay in the creek bottom or gain the bench—both options are good. After the dihedrals, head up the large gully—Cat in the Hat starts on the right wall of the gully and is completely hidden until you are near it. The use trail to Cat in the Hat is major and easy to find, and there are no cliff bands to be avoided, so any of the several trails up to the base will work. Most people take about 30 minutes for the approach. Hopefully climbers and the BLM will get together and consolidate the many trails into a single marked trail to help reduce erosion at this highly popular spot.

East Face of Mescalito

Follow the Cat in the Hat approach, but just past the fork in the canyon bottom, cut up right to the prow of the East Face.

Northeast Face of Mescalito

While hiking along the trail above the creekbed, keep an eye out for the Y2K/ Next Century formation (see photo). It is excellent black rock with several roofs. Once directly across from this area (about 200 yards before Dark Shadows), scramble down to the creek and up to the wall, crossing the creek near a huge log. Bushwack straight to the wall.

Mescalito North, Dark Shadows

While it is possible to thrash along the streambed of the right branch, it is much easier to gain the climbers' trail on the right bench. Just as a line of 40-foot-tall red cliffs seems to force you into the stream, climb up the bench and around a prominent huge boulder. A beautiful trail leads from here straight to Dark Shadows. (Thanks Access Fund volunteers!) Dark Shadows begins on a rock above a 6-foot waterfall between two pools of water.

Descent

Rap the routes, and reverse the approach. Please do not travel in the wash, the main trail was built specifically to reduce traffic in this sensitive riparian habitat, one of the few in Red Rocks which nearly always has flowing water.

Cat in the Hat 5.6★★★★

Time to climb route:	**2-3 hours**
Approach time:	**30 minutes**
Descent time:	**1.5 hours**
Sun exposure:	**mid-morning to afternoon**
Height of route:	**500'**

At first glance Cat in the Hat looks unimpressive. A nice first pitch crack leads to broken ledges, trees, and no obvious route. However, hidden above the trees are steep brown walls with awesome cracks, jugs, and a bit of slabby face. With great and consistent climbing, big belay ledges, and an easy rappel, Cat in the Hat is the most popular route of its grade in Red Rocks.

FA: Bruce Eisner, Joanne Urioste, 4/76.

History

Historically, Cat in the Hat marked the conversion of George and Joanne Urioste into "Red Rocks climbers." Even though they had arrived in Las Vegas a year and a half earlier, they had not done much local climbing. This was due to the unfavorable impressions of their first experiences. Thick, hostile flora, unsound rock, and oppressive heat combined to direct their climbing energies elsewhere.

In the spring of 1976 they started scouting the line that would shortly become Cat in the Hat. John Shirley, an airman stationed at nearby Nellis Air Force Base, accompanied them on the original reconnaissance. Miraculously, the climbing experience was the exact opposite of their previous misadventures. Brush was largely avoided. The rock was excellent. And the spring weather was perfect. To top it all off, the climbing was clean, aesthetic, and easier than expected.

Cat in the Hat	Pitch	1	2	3	4	5	6
Free difficulty	≥5.10						
	5.9						
	5.8						
	5.7						
	5.6	●			●		●
	≤5.5		●	●		●	

They climbed the varnished headwall on the sixth pitch and set up a belay on a tiny stance. The crack above petered out on a white sandstone slab. George led up and drilled the protection bolt that certainly has to be a contender for the title of "most clipped Red Rocks trad bolt." At the time, it was the only bolt on the route. Since it was getting late, and they were only halfway to the top, they retreated for the day. Ironically, schedule conflicts prevented George from participating on the summit day. Joanne teamed up with local climber Bruce Eisner to complete the final section of the route.

The high quality of the climbing on this route changed the Uriostes's opinion and resulted in renewed interest in the local climbing potential. Within a year they accomplished a number of significant first ascents including the Kaleidoscope Cracks, Lady Wilson's Cleavage, and several routes on Windy Peak.

– Larry DeAngelo

Strategy

With a sunny exposure and a short approach, Cat in the Hat usually has perfect climbing weather during prime season. That means crowds, and unfortunately the biggest hazard on the route is multiple parties—some going up, some down, and all getting ropes tangled. Thus, the best plan is to be there first—or to do it quickly late in the day.

It is well-protected in general, except for the last pitch, which has a moderate (5.5) slab runout above a bomber 1/2" bolt. However, those inexperienced at slab climbing sometimes decide to avoid the last pitch or retreat.

Like many rappels at Red Rocks, ropes can get stuck. Luckily, a new 5.10d bolted arête variation on the last pitch has an anchor in a perfect location to reduce the likelihood of a stuck rope on the rappel off the top anchor.

Retreat

Rappel the route. The route has good ledges and trees and is relatively well-protected in any sudden storm.

Rack

nuts: 1 set
cams: 2 ea .6-3"
      1 ea 4"
many slings

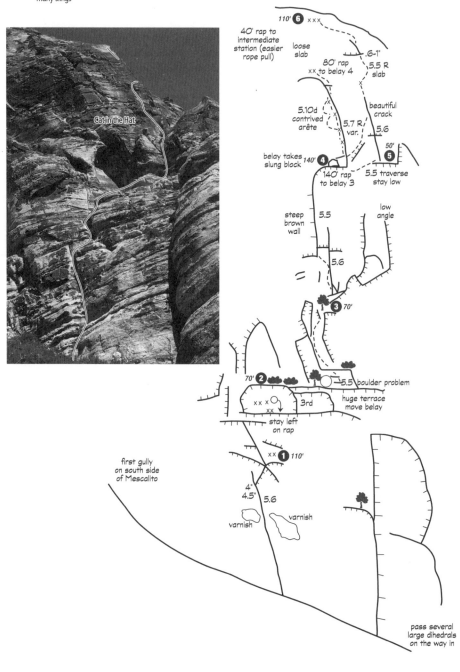

110' **6** x x x

40' rap to
intermediate
station (easier
rope pull)

loose
slab

.6-1"

80' rap
xx to belay 4

5.5 R
slab

beautiful
crack

5.10d
contrived
arête

5.7 R/
var.

5.6

belay takes
slung block

140' **4**

50'

140' rap
to belay 3

5.5 traverse
stay low

5

steep
brown
wall

5.5

low
angle

5.6

3 70'

70' **2**

5.5 boulder problem

x x x
xx

3rd

huge terrace
move belay

stay left
on rap

xx **1** 110'

first gully
on south side
of Mescalito

4"
4.5"

5.6

varnish

varnish

varnish

pass several
large dihedrals
on the way in

Cat in the Hat

Mescalito, East Face

Approach time: 30-45 minutes

Sun exposure: sunrise to mid-afternoon

Height of routes: 150-240'

The East Face of Mescalito is a beautiful black wall with a short approach, and with morning sun on black rock, it is great even on winter mornings.

A. Pine Nuts 5.10b R★★★

FA: Chris Gill, Paul Ross, Todd Swain, 12/98.

Excellent climbing up a steep black wall, Pine Nuts is reminiscent of Y2K, just around the corner. However, the first pitch is runout and loose, and the crux is pulling the lip of the roof on large delicate holds with poor protection (no fat bolt here!). Thus, the route is a far more serious undertaking than Y2K. Luckily, the awesome second pitch face is easily accessed by traversing left just after the roof on When A Stranger Calls, and then the first pitch of Pine Nuts can easily be toproped.

B. When A Stranger Calls 5.9★★★★

FA: Randy Grandstaff, Steve Anderson, 1981.

When A Stranger Calls has excellent and challenging climbing up steep huecos and through a roof. The crux is right off the deck—face climbing with intermittent pro in huecos—and is a tad runout. The route continues to the top of the wall, but the first pitch is the gem, and is easily rapped from a convoluted sling anchor to the right (also the top of This Ain't No Disco). Bring extra long slings to replace worn or old slings around several horns and constrictions.

C. This Ain't No Disco 5.8 R★★

FA: Randy Grandstaff, Randy Marsh, 1982.

This fun, challenging climb is on somewhat loose terrain with intermittent protection. It is a great route for those comfortable with routefinding, infrequent pro, and a bit of loose rock. Bring extra long slings to replace worn or old slings around several horns and constrictions at the anchor.

A. Pine Nuts 5.10b R★★★
nuts: 1 set; cams: 2 ea .5-1.25",

B. When A Stranger Calls 5.9★★★★
nuts: 1 set; cams: 1 ea .6-1.5", 4", 2 ea 2-3"

C. This Ain't No Disco 5.8 R★★
nuts: 1 set; cams: 1 ea .5-3"
two ropes required to rappel all routes

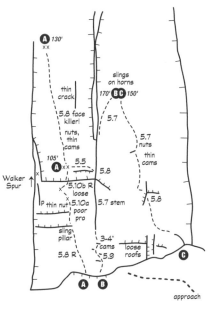

Y2K 5.10b★★★

Time to climb route:	**2-3 hours**
Approach time:	**45 minutes**
Descent time:	**1-1.5 hours**
Sun exposure:	**early morning (never in winter)**
Height of route:	**400'**

Y2K is a Red Rocks gem with awesome face climbing up steep black rock. With supplemental pro between widely spaced bolts, a huge roof with a fat bolt right at the lip, and endless perfect incut holds, Y2K is a great example of the beautiful rock that makes Red Rocks an international climbing destination.

FA: Todd Swain, Paul Ross, 11/98.

Strategy

Fairly popular, Y2K often has multiple parties, but it's easy to see if anyone is there from the approach trail to Dark Shadows, and a wide variety of other short routes is within a few minutes walk (Dark Shadows area, Pine Nuts area, and the Brass Wall). After the first two long pitches, which you wish will go on forever, the route traverses right around the corner into a dihedral, where the character abruptly changes. High in the dihedral is a great 5.9 stemming corner with only tiny micro nuts for protection. The rappel from this last pitch is a notorious rope eater, and many parties rappel after the first two pitches.

If there is a party ahead of you or you need a warm-up, consider doing the first pitch of The Next Century.

Retreat

Rap the route with two ropes. Use care when pulling ropes on the rap from the fourth pitch.

Y2K	Pitch 1	2	3	4
Free difficulty	≥5.10 ●			
	5.9			●
	5.8		●	
	5.7			
	5.6			
	≤5.5		●	

Greg Barnes

A. The Next Century 5.10d★★★

FA: Todd Swain, Paul Ross, 11/98.

With one of the single best pitches at Red Rocks, The Next Century is a stout challenge for the 5.10 leader. The long second pitch is everything you want in a testpiece: varied climbing, exposure, good but not trivial pro placements, and challenging and interesting moves.

The route is not that popular due to the difficult climbing, but The Next Century still sometimes has multiple parties. The first pitch (5.9) is a bit loose, but fun, and it can be done on its own with a single 60m rope. The second pitch is the business, as it starts off with a hard 5.10d thin edging slab between two not-too-closely spaced bolts. The endless awesome face and arête ends with an anchor hidden out of sight. Two ropes are required to rappel from the second pitch.

Y2K 5.10b★★★★
nuts: 2 ea micro, med, 1 ea sml, lrg
cams: 1 ea .5-2"

B. The Next Century 5.10d★★★★
nuts: 1 set
cams: 2 ea .4-.6", 1 ea .75-3"
many slings

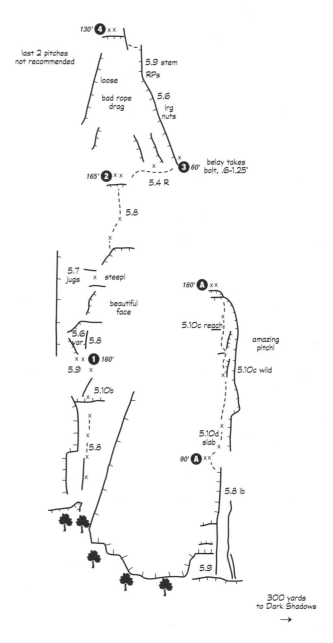

last 2 pitches
not recommended

130' **4** x x

5.9 stem
RPs

loose

bad rope
drag

5.6
lrg
nuts

165' **2** x x

x   **3** 60'   belay takes
5.4 R   bolt, .6-1.25"

x
5.8
x

5.7   x steep!   160' **A** x x
jugs
                                              x
          beautiful   5.10c reach
          face
                                                        amazing
5.6   pitch!
var. 5.8
                                 5.10c wild
x x **1** 160'
5.9 x

          5.10b
          x
          x
          x
        5.8   5.10d
          x   slab   x
                                 90' **A** x x
          x
                                              5.8 lb

                                 5.9

                                 300 yards
                                 to Dark Shadows
                                 →

Dark Shadows 5.8★★★★★

Time to climb route: **2 hours**

Approach time: **45 minutes**

Descent time: **1.5 hours**

Sun exposure: **rare morning sun**

Height of route: **1000'**

It's hard to believe that the steep, dark, and ominous dihedral of Dark Shadows is rated only 5.8. The route is capped by a huge roof and has walls so black and polished that they shine. Located in a tight canyon with large trees and pools of water, the atmosphere is distinctly unlike other Red Rocks climbs. While the route goes all the way to the top of Mescalito, it is rare for anyone to venture above the fourth pitch, especially when faced with the choice of a convenient rappel or a nasty and infamous descent from the top of the route. The only drawback to this amazing climb is the crowds…and the soaked ropes that are hard to avoid on the last rappel!

History

Back in the 1960s, this formation was known as Red Cap, and access was limited due to private property. Jeff Lansing was dating the caretaker's daughter and thus had the connection needed to get easily to the base of the routes. Both caretaker and daughter fit very well into the 1960s hippie psychedelic scene. When Jeff and Peter Wist climbed the East Face in 1968, they named the formation Mescalito, which had the proper hallucinogenic overtones.

As a friend of Jeff, Joe Herbst was able to include the Mescalito formation in the thorough scouting he applied to all the Red Rocks canyons. Joe's knowledge paid off

with first ascents of several good lines on Mescalito in the company of a number of Red Rocks regulars. The logical question is how did Joe miss such an obvious line as Dark Shadows? Joe says simply, "I don't know. There's a lot of rock out there—maybe we just didn't get around to it."

Joanne Urioste's 1984 guidebook credits Nick Nordblom and Jon Martinet with the first ascent of the complete route in 1979. Nick was fairly "old-school." He and a few friends did their initial climbing with a handful of Eiger oval carabiners, and a dacron rope liberated from its former function as the mainsheet on a friend's sailboat. Not quite starting with the family clothesline, but close. In the middle 1970s, Dark Shadows was a four pitch route leading up to the big roof. At that time the initial slab pitch had no protection bolts, but Nick and his partners climbed it anyway, wearing their heavy Vasque mountaineering boots. "Really good edging," said Nick.

On the day they started their complete ascent, Nick and Jon headed up the "short route" with just one 150-foot rope. The concept of going all the way to the top of the peak had not really formed in their minds. They reached the belay position under the large roof and evaluated their situation. With only one rope, the rappel option did not appeal to them. The alternative was to continue up to the summit. The decision was made and they continued up. They climbed another nine pitches wandering up the upper crack systems before they pulled onto the summit ridge. Their problems were not over. Neither of them was certain of the descent route. They bushwhacked through manzanita, scrambled, rappelled, and downclimbed, eventually reaching the north fork of Pine Creek. The arduous descent must have made an impression on Nick. Despite countless ascents at Red Rocks, he has never returned to the summit of Mescalito.

Dark Shadows	Pitch	1	2	3	4
Free difficulty	≥5.10				
	5.9				
	5.8				●
	5.7		●	●	
	5.6				
	≤5.5	●			

Nick had a mystery of his own. High on the wall, he and Jon found an old Cassin steel carabiner and a tattered scrap of webbing. Even back in the 1970s, this was not common hardware. I recently had the chance to ask Joe Herbst if he ever carried Cassin steel carabiners. "All the time," he said. "Usually used them as leavers."

– Larry DeAngelo

Strategy

An early start is one way to avoid a big line at Dark Shadows. Unfortunately, at present the gate to the loop road has limited hours often resulting in a race to the Pine Creek trailhead as soon as the gate opens. However, Dark Shadows is relatively short, and it is not uncommon to find no one there in early afternoon on a beautiful day.

The first pitch is "only 5.5," but is slab climbing on small, crumbly edges. Luckily, while somewhat runout, the two 1/4" bolts were replaced by the ASCA in 2001, and a relaxed attitude can help on the slab climbing. The second pitch has a bit of tricky liebacking, but great holds appear just in time. The third pitch has a few sections of awkward jamming/stemming, but juggy holds on the face offer relief high on the pitch. The fourth pitch is the crux, with one wide section of the crack that must be face climbed around, but it has great pro right before the crux and a very clean fall.

It's possible to toprope several hard climbs below the rappels on Dark Shadows, but care should be taken on rope length, and if it appears that you will interfere with others rappelling above you, it'd be best to descend.

Stronger leaders might consider rounding out the day on the first two pitches of Risky Business (5.10 R).

Retreat

Rappel to descend. One 60m rope will suffice, but you must be VERY careful on the first rappel—a backup method such as an autoblock is recommended. It is difficult to avoid getting the rope wet. Rappelling twice with a single rope from the second pitch will make it easier to keep ropes dry.

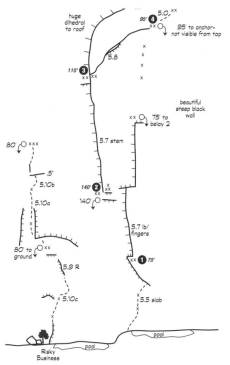

Rack

nuts: 1 ea sml
     2 ea med, lrg
cams: 2 ea .6-2"
     1 ea 2.5-4"

Brass Wall

Approach time: **30 minutes**

Sun exposure: **morning to afternoon**

Height of routes: **70' to 150'**

With quality cracks, a short approach, and a good concentration of moderate climbs, the Brass Wall is one of the most popular traditional crags at Red Rocks. In addition, black rock combined with a sunny exposure make the Brass Wall one of the warmest crags in the main canyons of Red Rocks.

The Brass Wall has sun all day and is usually perfect in the climbing high season, but can get too warm in hot spells. Varnishing Point, Topless Twins, and Straight Shooter are the classic must-do climbs and lines are not uncommon. Since most routes are very short, extended toproping by groups is a problem, so please be courteous.

Approach

As you hike up Pine Creek Canyon, about half way in to Dark Shadows and Cat in the Hat, the Brass Wall sits high on the right. Along a wide, flat section of trail about 200 yards before you see the canyon splitting, a small ridge of the hill to the right comes down to the trail. The approach trail for Brass Wall goes up this ridge, which heads up to the right edge of the small pink cliff band. Once on top, follow the trail over left; either head up to Straight Shooter Wall or continue until below Brass Wall. Do not attempt to downclimb the cliff band as loose blocks, steep drop-offs, and cacti await those trying to take a short-cut (which even if you successfully downclimb does not save any time).

Descent

Descend all routes by rappelling. Follow the same trail back to the car.

Sarah Felchlin

A	Sniveler	F	Serious Business
B	Heavy Spider Karma	G	Varnishing Point
C	Topless Twins	H	Simpatico
D	Mushroom People	I	Straight Shooter
E	No Laughing Matter		

A. Sniveler   5.6 R★★

FA: Unknown, circa 1980.

Fun, steep climbing through holes and horizontal cracks, Sniveler is a serious lead due to the loose protection and runouts. Climb way back right to the anchor of Topless Twins to descend.

B. Heavy Spider Karma   5.6★★★

FA: Unknown, circa 1980.

This is a beautiful thin hand crack to a slightly runout easy face. It is somewhat runout up top, especially if you break out right before the top of the crack, and care should be taken getting to the anchor.

C. Topless Twins   5.9★★★★

FA: Randal Grandstaff, Wendell "The Dean" Broussard, 1980.

Awesome climbing up angular crack/liebacks, finger cracks, and face to a convenient anchor—Topless Twins is popular for a reason.

D. Mushroom People   5.10d R★★★

FA: Dave Diegelman, Randal Grandstaff, Greg Child, 1979.

Mushroom People is highly recommended for those comfortable at the grade. It has great climbing, but is runout at the start and has a slick crux off of thin pro.

E. No Laughing Matter   5.10a★★★

FA: Greg Child, Randy Grandstaff, 1979.

No Laughing Matter gets its name from the large loose flakes and plates which make up the crux of the climb. This is a serious lead as you shouldn't pull out on certain holds; yet the protection is excellent, and with a helmeted belayer who is paying attention, there is not much to fear. A contrived 5.11a (Serious Business) can be toproped from the anchor, but amazingly, a link of the bottom of No Laughing Matter to the improbable-looking thin crack top of Serious Business is only 5.9 (but a bit runout and loose). The anchor is about 105 to 110 feet off the ledge, but if you rappel to the right into the "hole" next to the first pitch anchoring spot for Varnishing Point you can just make it with one 60m rope (but tie knots in both ends!).

F. Serious Business   5.11a R★

This is contrived and cruxy out the top of the roof at the start—a poor lead, but a fun toprope. The more logical route starts up No Laughing Matter and then goes right up the thin crack seam; this is 5.9 R and a reasonable lead for those comfortable on loose terrain. The anchor is shared with No Laughing Matter (see description for details).

G. Varnishing Point   5.8★★★★

FA: Joe Herbst, circa 1979.

Two short pitches, clean rock, and good pro make Varnishing Point highly popular. The rappel anchor is down and right from the top of the climb, but the downclimb is easy to a large ledge. A good 5.11 toprope is below, but because of the somewhat sharp edge, rope drag is usually pretty nasty. Please do not toprope if others are waiting to descend.

H. Simpatico   5.10a R★★★

FA: Jay Smith, Jo Bently, Jenni Stone, circa 1980.

Tricky climbing and thin pro off the deck lead up the shallow dihedral, and when you get to the roof the thin holds out right don't inspire confidence—until you find the jugs above the roof! There is no great pro at the roof crux, so care should be taken moving around to the right, especially as many of the jugs are somewhat hollow. Once on the ramp, either climb the runout arête, or stay in the corner and use stemming and offwidth technique.

I. Straight Shooter   5.9★★★★

FA: Joe Herbst, circa 1975.

Straight Shooter Wall is to the right of the huge gully (Beer & Ice Gully). When you get to the base you see why it gets so much traffic—the perfect splitter 5.9 finger crack. Several bolted 5.11s surround Straight Shooter, and it's easy to toprope the one to the right. There are no good feet at the crux, which requires cranking on finger locks, so if you haven't done this before it may feel hard for 5.9. Luckily, bomber pro makes it a perfect climb to learn on!

A. Sniveler 5.6 R ★★ nuts: 1 set; cams: 1 ea .6-3", screamers recommended

B. Heavy Spider Karma 5.6 ★★★★ nuts: 1 ea med, lrg; cams: 1 ea .6-.75", 1 ea 2-3", 2 ea 1-1.5" (extra 1.25")

C. Topless Twins 5.9 ★★★★ nuts: 1 set; cams: 2 ea .6-1.5", 1 ea 2-3"

D. Mushroom People 5.10d R ★★★★ nuts: 1 ea micro, med, lrg, 2 ea sml; cams: 2 ea .33-1", 1 ea 1.25-3"

E. No Laughing Matter 5.10a ★★★★ nuts: 1 set; cams: 2 ea .6-2", 1 ea 3"

F. Serious Business 5.11a R ★★★★ nuts: 2 sets; cams: 1 ea .5-1.5"

G. Varnishing Point 5.8 ★★★★ nuts: 1 set; cams: 1 ea .6-4"

H. Simpatico 5.10a R ★★★ nuts: 1 set; cams: 2 ea .33-1.25", 1 ea 1.5-3", optional: 1 ea 4-7"

I. Straight Shooter 5.9 ★★★★ nuts: 1 set; cams: 2 ea .6-1.5", 1 ea 2-2.5"

Dan McQuade and Will Gove on Pitch 11 of Original Route on Rainbow Wall (5.12). (Greg Epperson)

Willow Springs Area

A popular, short paved spur off the main Loop Road, the Willow Springs Area is known for old American Indian art and a small picnic area (with some good bouldering). The short cragging routes here are a quick and easy hike from the car. Ragged Edges Wall and the Case Face get early morning sun, while Hidden Falls Wall does not, but since the walls are right near the road and rarely get windy, they are often climbed even in colder weather.

Sarah Felchlin

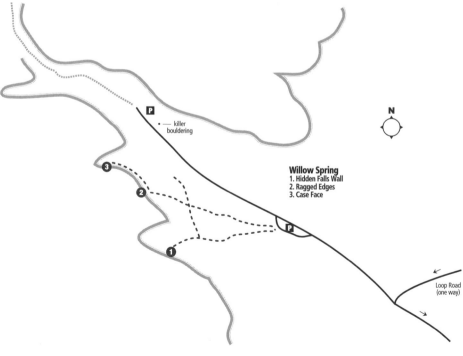

killer bouldering

Willow Spring
1. Hidden Falls Wall
2. Ragged Edges
3. Case Face

N

Loop Road (one way)

Hidden Falls Wall
Ragged Edges Wall

Approach time: **10 minutes**

Sun exposure: **morning to noon**

Height of routes: **100' to 200'**

Hidden Falls Wall

The Ragged Edges area in Willow Springs is the most accessible crag in the main canyons at Red Rocks. Ragged Edges itself is a near-vertical two-pitch 5.8 with a wild hand, fist, and offwidth crack usually bypassed via stemming and face climbing.

Only a few hundred yards from the road, these climbs are popular when the weather is appropriate. Because they are generally shady, they can be cold, although Ragged Edges cliff gets morning sun.

Approach

Park at the big parking lot on the left about 100 yards up the Willow Spring Road from the main Loop Road. Take the right trail to get to Ragged Edges (the very dark rock crag on the right), or the left trail to get to Hidden Falls Wall (black wall on the left about 100 yards before the waterfall/alcove).

Descent

From the top of Ragged Edges cliff, walk off right around the crag on easy slabs and trail. All other climbs are rappelled.

A. Left Out   5.10d★★★★

FA: Joe Herbst, circa 1975.

Sweet climbing up a slightly overhanging wall, Left Out doesn't really have a 5.10d crux, but the pump factor wears you down. Overhung huecos at the start (protected by a 3-inch cam in a hueco) lead to tricky stemming/fingers, a great hand crack, then a committing lieback section. Higher, you move out of the crack onto face which looks runout—until you find the bomber finger crack in a few feet. The anchor of a new hard route to the right makes for a convenient rappel.

B. Unknown

Very hard and thin sport climb.

C. Black Track   5.9★★★

FA: Joe Herbst, early 1970s.

Awkward but well-protected hand, fist, and offwidth up a ramp. A great crack to build technique. You can toprope a few face climbs from the anchor.

D. Unknown

Highly contrived and a squeeze job—difficulty depends on how close you follow the bolts, which are currently chopped.

E. Bigfoot   5.10a★★★

Great face climbing and a tad runout.

F. Buffalo Balls   5.11c★

FA: (TR) Bob Yoho, 1989; (Lead) Don Burroughs, Alan Busby, 1992.

Short overhung sport climb, with a reachy crux.

G. Kemosabe   5.10a R★★

FA: Sal Mamusia, Richard Harrison, Paul Van Betten, Wendell Broussard, 1983.

Tricky slabby climbing, but at least the bolt is good now.

H. Tonto   5.5★★★

FA: Joe and Betsy Herbst, 1972.

Low-angle but fun, the climb goes right on the face to avoid the roof. You can rap from the tree with two ropes, or walk off around Ragged Edges in only a few minutes.

I. Vision Quest   5.12d★★

FA: Paul Van Betten, Sal Mamusia, 1988.

Short and very hard. There are two bolts down and right which are from an abandoned project.

J. Bodiddly   5.10c R★★★

FA: Robert Finlay, Richard Harrison, 1985.

Good climbing, but runout.

K. Plan F   5.10a★★★ or 5.11 R★★

FA: Paul Van Betten, Richard Harrison, Sal Mamusia, Nick Nordblom, 1983.

The first section is easily toproped from Ragged Edges, but be careful since the crux is in a bad spot for a pendulum. A great lead because the crux is at the top. Few try the runout 5.11 finish.

L. Ragged Edges   5.8★★★★★

FA: Joe Herbst, early 1970s.

The classic climb of the area. Great hands on the first pitch, then a short burly fist section followed by lots of stemming and face climbing around a wide crack. Runout without large cams, but thin pro can be had in horizontals. The first pitch is a great place to practice hand jamming in the smooth, slick rock. You can toprope the first section of Plan F, but please be considerate of others wishing to climb Ragged Edges (or Plan F).

M. Chicken Eruptus   5.10b★★★★

FA: Paul Van Betten, Wendell Broussard, Richard Harrison, Sal Mamusia, 1983.

Killer climbing, but a bit runout. Two bolts plus lots of thinner pro in horizontals protect a wild, exposed climb.

Ragged Edges Wall

A. **Left Out 5.10d**★★★★ nuts: 1 set; cams: 2 ea .6-3"

B. **Unknown** many quickdraws

C. **Black Track 5.9**★★★ nuts: 1 ea med, lrg; cams: 1 ea .6-1.5", 4", 2 ea 2-3", more 2-4" if you have them

D. **Unknown**

E. **Bigfoot 5.10a**★★★ 4 quickdraws

F. **Buffalo Balls 5.11c**★ 4 quickdraws

G. **Kemosabe 5.10a R**★★ nuts: 1 ea micro, med, 2 ea sml; cams: 2 ea .33-1", 1 ea 1.25-1.5"

H. **Tonto 5.5**★★★ nuts: 1 set; cams: 1 ea .6-.75", 2 ea 1-2", 1 ea 3"

I. **Vision Quest 5.12d**★★ 4 quickdraws

J. **Bodidily 5.10c R**★★★ nuts: 1 set; cams: 2 ea .6-1.25", 1 ea 1.5-3"

K. **Plan F 5.10a**★★★ **or 5.11 R**★★ nuts: 1 set; cams: 2 ea .4-1.25", 1 ea 1.5-2"

L. **Ragged Edges 5.8**★★★★ nuts: 1 set; cams: 2 ea .6-4", 1 ea 4.5-7" (more if desired)

M. **Chicken Eruptus 5.10b**★★★★ nuts: 1 set; cams: 2 ea .4-2", 1 ea 3"

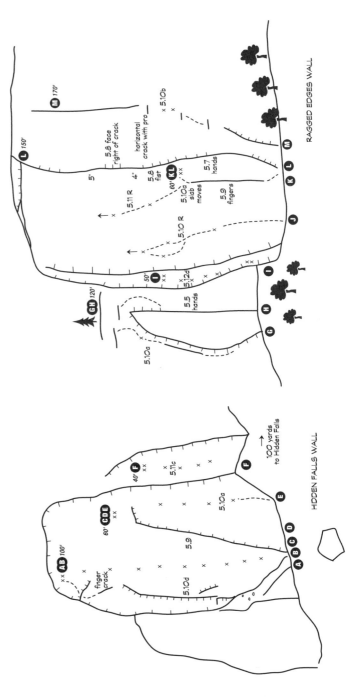

RAGGED EDGES WALL

HIDDEN FALLS WALL

100 yards to Hidden Falls

Case Face

Approach time: 15 minutes

Sun exposure: sunrise to mid-morning

Height of routes: 80'

Case Face is a short, white wall with several fun routes about 300 yards up and right from Ragged Edges Wall. This wall, like Ragged Edges, only gets early morning sun.

Matthew Schutz leading Head Case, Case Face.

Approach

Park at the big parking lot on the left about 100 yards up the Willow Spring Road from the main Loop Road. Take the right trail to get to Ragged Edges (the dark crag on the right). Once at Ragged Edges Wall, hike up and right for 300 yards to the next cliff—Case Face.

Descent

Rappel 70 feet with one rope and reverse the approach. It takes about 15 minutes to get to the car.

A. Just In Case   5.5★

FA: Donette Swain, Todd Swain, George Reid, Catriona Reid, 10/94.

A steep and challenging start past a bolt soon eases to trivial terrain with poor protection.

B. Space Case   5.7★

FA: Randy Marsh, Pauline Schroeder, 1983.

A tricky section past a bolt soon eases into easy climbing up a low-angle crack. Note that the first ascent was done without the bolt.

C. Head Case   5.9★★★

FA: Todd Swain, Donette Swain, George Reid, Catriona Reid, 1994.

An excellent face climb with knobs and edges, Head Case is the best climb at the crag. A slung horn between the second and third bolts, plus thin cams at the top, make this a well-protected lead.

Lynn Hill focuses on Red Skies, The Fixx Cliff (5.11+). (Greg Epperson)

D. Hard Case   5.9★★

FA: Joe Herbst, Matt McMackin, mid-1970s.

The first climb at the crag, Hard Case is a fun but awkward crack through a roof, with a section of easy face climbing gaining the anchor.

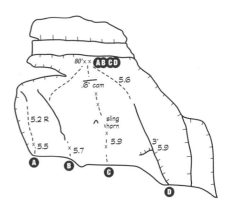

A. Just in Case 5.5★ cams: 1 ea .6-3"

B. Space Case 5.7★ cams: 1 ea .6-3"

C. Head Case 5.9★★★ cams: 1 ea .6", sling for horn

D. Hard Case 5.9★★ nuts: 1 set; cams: 1 ea .6-3", optional 1.5-3"

White Rock Spring

White Rock Spring is the first "canyon" you reach on the Loop Road. With open desert on one side and the large, white Angel Food Wall on the other, it's not particularly spectacular compared to the huge walls behind it. But as is often the case at Red Rocks, the scale is deceptive, and with a fairly short and easy approach, plus fun moderate climbs, it is a popular destination.

Greg Barnes

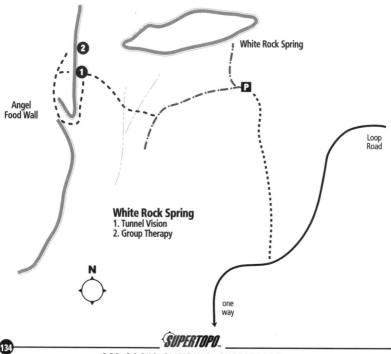

White Rock Spring
1. Tunnel Vision
2. Group Therapy

N

Angel Food Wall

Greg Barnes

Angel Food Wall is the first major formation encountered going around the Loop Road past the sport climbing areas. It appears to be small, but the scale of the main escarpment behind it is deceiving. Slanting wide crack and chimney systems between fins of white rock also look uninviting, but the abundant face holds make the climbing supremely fun. The approach is short by Red Rocks standards, and with multiple routes in the 5.7 range, Angel Food Wall is very popular.

Approach

Hike down the old road from the White Rock Spring parking area (at the end of a short, but rough, gravel spur off the main Loop Road). Take the well-worn trail to the right when the road turns left and follow it up through a short bouldery streambed. Many trails lead up left to the base of the wall; please try to stay on the most heavily used (hopefully some trail consolidation work will be done here).

The trails lead to the base of Tunnel Vision, which traverses under a large roof only 15 feet up to gain a low-angle dihedral. Group Therapy starts about 150 yards to the right of Tunnel Vision from boulders at the base of large trees, on the lower left wall of a huge shady chimney/recess.

Descent

From the top of Tunnel Vision, drop down in the large 3rd class chimney and follow it left to a large terrace. Hike around into a gully, and either rappel 50 feet from slings around a large block, or hike up 20 feet and over into the next gully and descend there (3rd/4th class). Descend following cairns, past numerous short 3rd class drop-offs, boulder scrambling, and a lot of annoying oak trees and cacti. Swing around to the base to pick up gear. It will save you about 10-20 minutes if you don't leave gear at the base, but on the other hand the best trail back is to traverse all the way to the trail you hiked up on.

To descend Group Therapy, go down the big 3rd class chimney, which joins the start of the Tunnel Vision descent after crawling under a huge chockstone.

Tunnel Vision 5.7 R★★★★★

Time to climb route: **4-6 hours**

Approach time: **30 minutes**

Descent time: **1 hour**

Sun exposure: **early morning**

Height of route: **700'**

Awesome, juggy face climbing and stemming up a fearsome looking chimney system, Tunnel Vision is great fun and a good introduction to easy chimney climbing. However, as with most chimney climbs, there is poor protection for long stretches, including the crux 5.7 pitch. The tunnel itself is a blast on polished rock which will make you nervous, but never gets too hard. Several variations including a new one on the crux pitch offer even more variety on an already sweet climb.

FA: Joe Herbst, Randal Grandstaff, 1974.

History

Tunnel Vision marked the beginning of an age of expansion in Red Rocks climbing. The previous year saw ascents of both the Rainbow Wall and Velvet Wall. Both climbs were achieved by parties that included Joe Herbst. Several years earlier, Joe adopted the clean climbing ethic while working with the influential Doug Robinson. As a leading figure in those days at Red Rocks, Joe passed on this influence to the next wave of climbers.

One impressionable youth who really picked up the ball and ran with it was young Randal Grandstaff. Just 16 years old at the time of the Tunnel Vision climb, Randal was at the beginning of a productive climbing career. His resume would soon include numerous significant Red Rocks ascents, many big Yosemite routes, and

even extended to an Everest expedition. Perhaps his greatest achievement was the establishment of the Sky's the Limit guide service. Randal's efforts put guiding on the map in Las Vegas and allowed him to make a living doing what he loved.

As if to complete some kind of cosmic great circle, Doug Robinson grew to know Randal well in the career they both shared. Doug observed, "Randal was a great guide. He was the kind of person who could inspire a client, who could help them to have their greatest experiences in the mountains. He had the ability to sense what his clients needed. He could fit in at a laid back climber's camp, then turn around and command the respect of the Special Forces troops he trained for the U.S. military." Randal died in a tragic rappelling accident in 2002.

– Larry DeAngelo

Strategy

Tunnel Vision usually has a line, and slow parties are very common as inexperienced leaders face the frightening prospect of running it out on chimney climbing.

Right off the deck is a short corner followed by a bouldery traverse to the right. While the pitch is rated 5.7, if high on a route this boulder problem might rate 5.8, so use a spotter and be careful.

To protect the climb well at the crux on the third pitch, large gear would be needed (#4 and #5 Big Bros), but would be difficult to place. A few good nut and okay thin cam placements can be used. Better to climb confidently and calmly through the runouts, and to rely on the great stems for rests. The crux section is wild—stemming past a narrow chimney that has an amazing flake at one edge to lieback.

As with other routes on this wall, great protection in small pockets can be found for tri-cams or narrow cams.

Retreat

You can retreat from any point on the first half of the climb by leaving long slings threaded through natural arches or around blocks. There is a bolted anchor as well on top of Pitch 2.

Tunnel Vision		Pitch 1	2	3	4	5	6
Free difficulty	≥5.10						
	5.9						
	5.8						
	5.7	●	●				●
	5.6				●		
	≤5.5	●		●			

Group Therapy 5.7 R★★★

Time to climb route:	**4-6 hours**
Approach time:	**30 minutes**
Descent time:	**1 hour**
Sun exposure:	**sunrise to mid-morning**
Height of route:	**700'**

Group Therapy has a wide offwidth crack pitch and a fearsome looking roof up high as it ascends a crack system out on a wide face. Group Therapy is the only climb in the area which gets much sun on the actual route. The roof is even more intimidating once you get to it, but is wild, fun climbing on good holds. Still, retreat from right before the roof is common as leaders face the frighteningly exposed climbing.

FA: Joe Herbst, Betsy Herbst, Randal Grandstaff, Matt McMackin, 1974.

History

The first ascent of Tunnel Vision went so well that Joe and Randy returned the following weekend. This time the team was expanded to include Joe's wife, Betsy, and Randy's high school buddy, Matt McMackin.

Joe says, "At the time, we were still working out what we could trust for protection in the sandstone. We felt pretty secure in the wide cracks, because that was mostly what we were climbing in Yosemite, so that's what seemed like the safest kind of route in Red Rocks. Besides, we thought Yosemite was 'real climbing' and we wanted to replicate that part of the experience, too."

The route turned out to be a pleasure. The weather was perfect. The companionship was first-rate. Those wide cracks were mild enough to be fun. There were comfortable ledges to accommodate their large first ascent party. All in all, the quality of the day rose above pleasant, the entire Group agreed, and achieved the level of Therapeutic.

– Larry DeAngelo

Strategy

While not as popular as Tunnel Vision, Group Therapy still gets lines, and an early start is recommended. Large gear is needed to protect the climb well, but often it goes beyond cams (currently available only to 7") into the realm of larger Big Bros.

It is not unreasonable to lead the climb with a normal rack, but the second pitch has no solid pro for a long stretch, and some experience on low-angle offwidths is needed. Loose flakes form the inside of the crack, and it is important not to pull out on them and to treat them gently as footholds.

The roof is huge and wild, but there are great face holds inside the narrow chimney which splits it, and medium to large cams protect it well. Above the roof is a long stretch of stemming and face climbing around the offwidth/chimney, and protection is scarce (again, #4 and #5 Big Bros could be used).

With the two harder pitches both run-out, and combined with some loose rock, Group Therapy is a fun but serious outing.

Retreat

Gear must be left to retreat from the route. Cams would probably have to be used at the base of the roof, while lower on the climb, nuts, a tree, and natural threads/slung horns could be used. Two ropes would be required to rappel past the second pitch offwidth.

Group Therapy	Pitch	1	2	3	4	5	6
Free difficulty	≥5.10						
	5.9						
	5.8						
	5.7	●					●
	5.6	●					
	≤5.5			●	●	●	

A. Tunnel Vision 5.7 R★★★★★
nuts: 1 set
cams: 1 ea .4-.5", 2 ea .6-1.5", 1 ea 2-4"
optional: #4 Big Bro, #.5, #1 tri-cams useful
many slings

B. Group Therapy 5.7 R★★★
nuts: 1 ea sml, med, 2 ea lrg
cams: 1 ea .5-2", 2 ea 2.5-4", 1 ea 4.5-7"
optional: #4 Big Bro, #.5, #1, #1.5 tri-cams useful
many slings

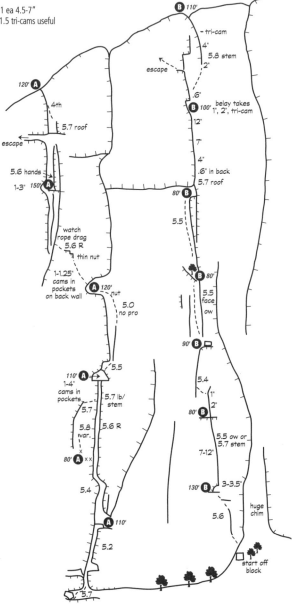

Tony Sartin climbing in the Calico Hills. (Greg Epperson)

Calico Hills

The Gallery

Great Red Book

Magic Bus

Greg Barnes

The Calico Hills are the large red and white hills to the north of Highway 159 before the start of the Loop Road, and on your right as you head up past the first two parking areas on the Loop Road ("First Pullout" and "Second Pullout" to climbers). The bright red Calico Hills were largely ignored by early Red Rocks climbers because of the soft rock and short routes. A complex series of small rock formations, the Calico Hills are akin to a sandstone version of the photogenic formations of Joshua Tree. Within this jumble of rocks are nearly all the sport climbs in Red Rocks, some excellent bouldering, and a smattering of shorter traditional climbs.

The first access to the area is the Calico Basin Road, which leads to the Red Spring Picnic Area (an access for some fun winter short trad climbs), then into dozens of private houses. Climbers have caused our own access problems here by parking on private property, annoying residents, and generally not keeping a low profile. The excellent Kraft boulders, covered with easy, moderate, and harder boulder problems with great landings, are on the opposite side of all the houses from the Red Spring Picnic Area. The best way to approach is to park at or near Red Spring Picnic Area, then hike along the west side of the houses on the large gravel road, then hike straight to the main south-facing escarpment staying on the roads. Here, join a trail along the escarpment and hike to the right, where the Kraft boulders are strewn along a half mile of the base. There are a few other parking areas here used to access crags and boulders. These may or may not be open— be intelligent about using them and respect the local residents!

The second access is the Loop Road. The Calico Hills have three large parking areas with bathrooms spaced along a few miles: the First Pullout, the Second Pullout, and the Sandstone Quarry. All have excellent winter sport climbing, covered extensively in other guidebooks (see the Introduction for details). In the SuperTopo, we include a sampling of sport climbs at The Gallery and Magic Bus that are warm on the coldest winter days (as long as there is sun), plus the fun two-pitch traditional route Great Red Book. All these areas are accessed from the Second Pullout. These pullouts fill completely in high season, and an early start is recommended to secure parking. See each area in the next few pages for approach and descent information.

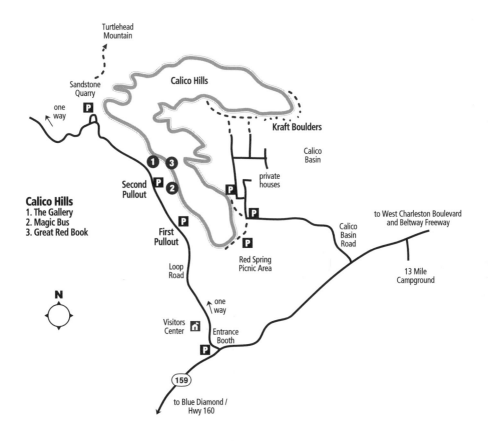

Turtlehead
Mountain

Calico Hills

Sandstone
Quarry

one
way

P

Kraft Boulders

Calico
Basin

**Second
Pullout**

1 3

P 2

private
houses

P

Calico Hills
1. The Gallery
2. Magic Bus
3. Great Red Book

P

to West Charleston Boulevard
and Beltway Freeway

**First
Pullout**

P

Calico
Basin
Road

P

13 Mile
Campground

Loop
Road

Red Spring
Picnic Area

N

one
way

Visitors
Center

Entrance
Booth

P

159

to Blue Diamond /
Hwy 160

The Gallery

Approach time: 20-30 minutes

Sun exposure: mid-morning to sunset

Height of routes: 30' to 80'

The Gallery is the most popular crag at Red Rocks, yet it is hard to spot among the huge convoluted wall of the Calico Hills. Perfect incut jugs, short and accessible routes, perfect warm weather even in mid-winter, and a huge lunch/hangout ledge make this a great climbing spot. The routes range from short to long and overhung, with the easier grade routes on the very short side.

Approach

Despite being easily visible from the parking lot, the approach to the Gallery has flummoxed more than a few people. Hike down the main trail from the parking lot, taking the left branch after 50 yards. This goes up over a small hill and descends gradually to the wash. Once at the wash, scramble up easy slabs opposite the end of the trail, following a heavily trafficked path which works up and left along one of the ridges (stay on the ridge and out of the gully). Follow this to the left, all the way past The Gallery (don't try to cut up early!), then scramble past the end of the gully and up to the far left end of The Gallery. Routes are listed from left to right.

Descent

Rappel all routes and reverse the approach.

A. Range of Motion   5.10d★★

FA: Todd Swain, Dick Peterson, Peggy Buckey, 5/90.

B. Sport Climbing is Neither   5.8★★

FA: Unknown, 1991.

Greg Barnes

C. Buck's Muscle World   5.9★★

FA: Greg Mayer, 1990.

D. Gelatin Pooch   5.10a★

FA: Greg Mayer, 1990.

E. Pump First, Pay Later   5.10b★★

FA: Greg Mayer, 1990.

F. Running Amuck   5.10c★★

FA: Greg Mayer, 1990.

G. Gridlock   5.11b★

FA: Greg Mayer, 1990.

H. Social Disorder   5.11d★

FA: Scott (aka Jimmy Dean), "Bucky" Bullock, Jonathan Knight, 1991.

I. A Day in the Life   5.11b★★

FA: Bill Boyle, 1989/90.

J. Minstrel in the Gallery   5.12b★

FA: Mike Tupper, 1989/90.

K. Yaak Crack   5.11d★★★

FA: Bill Boyle, 1989/90

L. The Gift   5.12c★★★

FA: Boone Speed, 1989/90.

Don Welsch on Nothing Shocking, The Gallery (5.13). (Greg Epperson)

Fear and Loathing (5.12a)

Wall of Confusion

5.10d   huecos

more overhanging 5.12-5.13 climbs →

Magic Bus

Approach time: 20-30 minutes

Sun exposure: mid-morning to sunset

Height of routes: 60'

Magic Bus is a huge block of great red and black sandstone, perched on a rocky hillside opposite the parking for the Second Pullout. With a small collection of excellent routes, including probably the most tightly bolted 5.8 at Red Rocks, it is very popular. In addition, it has a crack route which serves as a great introduction to thinner cracks on longer routes at Red Rocks. Since it is directly across from the parking area, it's easy to see if the crag is already occupied by a large group.

Approach

There are two normal approaches for Magic Bus. The first is the direct approach up a few gullies straight to the crag, which involves some 4th class scrambling that can be tricky.

The much better approach is to head left, then follow a ramp system back up to the crag. First, hike down the trail to the main wash below the parking lot. Head left, and up a smaller rocky wash for 100 yards past some water holes (sometimes dry)—this involves some 3rd class scrambling (watch out for sand or gravel on the rock). Just past this short rocky section, turn sharply right and scramble up the ramp past bushes and boulders, all the way to the Magic Bus. There is nothing difficult on this ramp, so if contemplating anything 4th class or harder, look for the easier way.

Descent

Rappel the routes, reverse the approach.

A. Electric Koolaid   5.9★★

FA: Donnette Swain, Todd Swain, 1994.

Fun climbing up the left edge of the wall, Electric Koolaid warrants caution due to somewhat loose holds. Most of the rock is good, but make sure to pull down (not out) on any hold that appears too suspicious.

Greg Barnes

B. Blonde Dwarf   5.9★★★

FA: Nick Nordblom, Paul Van Betten, 1988.

A great thin crack to a short steep face, Blonde Dwarf is a good introduction to thin cracks on Red Rocks multi-pitch climbs. The crack is relatively low angle and not harder than 5.7, with the crux face at the top protected by bolts.

C. Neon Sunset   5.8★★★

Fun face climbing with lots of bolts, Neon Sunset is a great little route, if perhaps overbolted. While it's a common first lead, always take care with the basics of rope management and leading, as this was the site of a fatal accident a few years ago.

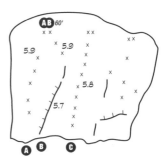

A. Electric Koolaid 5.9★★ 5 quickdraws

B. Blonde Dwarf 5.9★★★ nuts: 1 set; cams: 2 ea .4-1". 1 ea 1.25"

C. Neon Sunset 5.8★★★ 9 quickdraws

Great Red Book 5.8 R★★★

Time to climb route:	**1-2 hours**
Approach time:	**30-45 minutes**
Descent time:	**30-45 minutes**
Sun exposure:	**afternoon**
Height of route:	**250'**

Sunny and warm, the Calico Hills are sought after by sport climbers. Great Red Book is the obvious left-leaning dihedral on the rocks above the Black Corridor area, and is one of the few traditional climbs in the area. The route is fairly short, and is a great introduction to the more traditionally protected faces and corners found on longer trad routes in Red Rocks.

FA: John Williamson and Bob Logerquist, 10/71.

Approach

Park at the Second Pullout and follow the main trail down toward the wash. Take the first right turn, then go left up the wash for 50 yards, and scramble up the gully past some pools. From here, head straight into and through the Black Corridor, the infamously grid-bolted but really fun sport climbing hot spot. After the corridor (which has a scramble up a drop-off midway through), go right up the gully and scree slope to the base of Great Red Book.

Descent

From the top, hike 20 yards to the right, then cut back down the big gully to your pack. Reverse the approach hike.

History

John Williamson was one of Red Rocks' earliest pioneers. In addition to several committing mountaineering exploits, he is responsible for a number of recorded short climbs. John seems to have had an affinity for interesting dihedrals in reddish rock. In addition to the Great Red Book, he also put up The Fox, the Nevada Book, and Red Riding Hood.

The Great Red Book line that is normally climbed today is not the line of the original ascent. Contemporary climbers wander out of the dihedral and face climb past several bolts, whereas the first ascentionists proceeded straight up the corner. George and Joanne Urioste established the more relaxed variation.

– *Larry DeAngelo*

Strategy

The crux of Great Red Book is finding a parking spot. Start early, or late, or you may have to deal with the overflow parking along the road itself.

The first pitch wanders up the face about 20 feet left of the corner, although some choose the much more difficult but well-protected climbing in the book itself. Climb slowly and look for protection options. Beware of some loose rock.

Retreat

You can rappel from the first pitch anchor. Someone installed bolts on the summit, but they are far back from the rounded edge and should not be used to rappel.

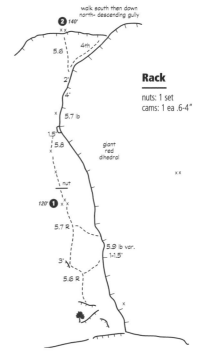

Rack

nuts: 1 set
cams: 1 ea .6-4"

We need YOUR feedback

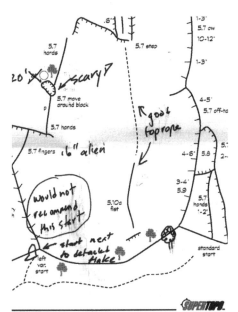

I love getting feedback on SuperTopos. The reason we make SuperTopos is so that you and other climbers can have an incredible experience on the rock. If there is any way I can make this experience better I want to know.

Every time you climb a route you will come away with a unique familiarity about each pitch. I want to hear what you thought of the climb and what you think can be improved on our topos. This information will help us make better topos and enhance other people's climbing experience.

FOR CURRENT ROUTE INFORMATION, V

Mail us your topo corrections and help make SuperTopos even better.

You will greatly help us if after your climb you do one of two things:

- Visit the web site's Climber Beta section (www.supertopo.com/route_beta) and tell SuperTopo users about the climb. What were the conditions like? Is there any extra beta? What did you think of the route?

- If you have any suggestions please email me at chris@supertopo.com or send snail mail to 2 Bradford Way, Mill Valley, CA 94941. Let me know if we got a pitch length wrong, if you disagreed with a rating, or if you think the topo could be better in any way.

Thank you for helping us improve SuperTopo,

Chris McNamara
Founder and CEO
SuperTopo

Beth Renn cruises up Blanc Czech, Meat Puppets Wall (5.11). (Greg Epperson)

Climbs by Rating

5.1 – 5.5

- ☐ Solar Slab Gully 5.3★★★ (94)
- ☐ Just in Case 5.5★ (133)
- ☐ Tonto 5.5★★★ (130)
- ☐ Unknown 5.5★★★ (43)

5.6

- ☐ Cat in the Hat 5.6★★★★ (117)
- ☐ Doobie Dance 5.6★★★★ (72)
- ☐ Geronimo 5.6★★★★ (107)
- ☐ Going Nuts 5.6★★★★ (96)
- ☐ Heavy Spider Karma 5.6★★★ (125)
- ☐ Jackass Flats 5.6★★ (30)
- ☐ Johnny Vegas 5.6 R★★★★★ (94)
- ☐ Lazy Buttress 5.6 R★★ (43)
- ☐ Sniveler 5.6 R★★ (125)
- ☐ Solar Slab 5.6★★★★★ (96)

5.7

- ☐ Group Therapy 5.7 R★★★ (137)
- ☐ Olive Oil 5.7 R★★★★★ (109)
- ☐ One-Armed Bandit 5.7 R★★ (110)
- ☐ Romper Room 5.7★★★★ (72)
- ☐ Schaeffer's Delight 5.7★★★★ (43)
- ☐ Space Case 5.7★ (133)
- ☐ Tunnel Vision 5.7 R★★★★★ (136)

5.8

- ☐ Blockade Runner 5.8★★★★ (30)
- ☐ Crimson Chrysalis 5.8★★★★★ (103)
- ☐ Dark Shadows 5.8★★★★★ (122)
- ☐ Frogland 5.8★★★★★ (42)
- ☐ Great Red Book 5.8 R★★★ (145)
- ☐ Lotta Balls 5.8★★★★★ (71)
- ☐ Neon Sunset 5.8★★★ (144)
- ☐ Ragged Edges 5.8★★★★★ (130)
- ☐ Sport Climbing is Neither 5.8★★ (143)
- ☐ This Ain't No Disco 5.8 R★★ (119)
- ☐ Unknown 5.8★★★ (43)
- ☐ Varnishing Point 5.8★★★★ (125)

5.9

- ☐ Aquarium 5.9 R★★★ (114)
- ☐ Arrow Place 5.9★★★★ (67)
- ☐ Beulah's Book 5.9★★★★ (93)
- ☐ Black Track 5.9★★★ (129)
- ☐ Blonde Dwarf 5.9★★★ (144)
- ☐ Buck's Muscle World 5.9★★ (143)
- ☐ Chuckwalla 5.9★★★★★ (36)
- ☐ Diet Delight 5.9★★★ (29)
- ☐ Electric Koolaid 5.9★★ (144)
- ☐ Epinephrine 5.9★★★★★ (62)
- ☐ Hard Case 5.9★★ (133)
- ☐ Head Case 5.9★★★ (133)
- ☐ Straight Shooter 5.9★★★★ (125)
- ☐ The Misunderstanding 5.9★★★ (46)
- ☐ Topless Twins 5.9★★★★ (125)
- ☐ When A Stranger Calls 5.9★★★★ (119)

5.10a

- ☐ Bigfoot 5.10a★★★ (129)
- ☐ Black Orpheus 5.10a★★★★ (88)
- ☐ Dream of Wild Turkeys 5.10a★★★★★ (55)
- ☐ Friendship Route 5.10a★★ (72)
- ☐ Gelatin Pooch 5.10a★ (143)
- ☐ Horndogger Select to Sundog 5.10a★★★ (98)
- ☐ Kemosabe 5.10a R★★ (130)
- ☐ No Laughing Matter 5.10a★★★ (125)
- ☐ Overhanging Hangover 5.10a★★★★ (61)
- ☐ Rob Roy 5.10a R★★★★ (72)
- ☐ Sand Felipe 5.10a★★★ (47)
- ☐ Simpatico 5.10a R★★★ (125)
- ☐ Sour Mash 5.10a★★★★★ (60)
- ☐ The Gobbler 5.10a★★★★ (58)
- ☐ Wholesome Fullback 5.10a★★★★★ (48)
- ☐ Plan F 5.10a★★★ (130)

5.10b

- ☐ Chicken Eruptus 5.10b★★★★ (130)
- ☐ Pine Nuts 5.10b R★★★ (119)
- ☐ Pump First, Pay Later 5.10b★★ (143)
- ☐ Y2K 5.10b★★★★ (120)
- ☐ Yellow Brick Road 5.10b★★★★★ (57)

5.10c

☐ Gin Ricky 5.10c★★★ (71)
☐ Prince of Darkness 5.10c★★★★★ (54)
☐ Running Amuck 5.10c★★ (143)
☐ Triassic Sands 5.10c★★★★★ (47)
☐ Bodiddly 5.10c R★★★ (130)
☐ Eagle Dance 5.10c A0★★★★ (77)

5.10d

☐ Left Out 5.10d★★★★ (129)
☐ Our Father 5.10d★★★ (48)
☐ Mai Tai 5.10d R★★★★ (72)
☐ Mazatlan 5.10d R★★★★ (46)
☐ Mushroom People 5.10d R★★★ (125)
☐ Range of Motion 5.10d★★ (143)
☐ Ringtail 5.10d★★★ (84)
☐ The Next Century 5.10d★★★★ (120)

5.11a

☐ Serious Business 5.11a R★ (125)

5.11b

☐ A Day in the Life 5.11b★★ (143)
☐ Gridlock 5.11b★ (143)

5.11c

☐ Buffalo Balls 5.11c★ (129)
☐ Ixtlan 5.11c★★★★ (46)
☐ Levitation 29 5.11c★★★★★ (80)
☐ Only the Good Die Young
5.11c★★★★ (50)

5.11d

☐ Social Disorder 5.11d★ (143)
☐ Yaak Crack 5.11d★★★ (143)

5.12a – 5.12d

☐ Minstrel in the Gallery 5.12b★ (143)
☐ The Gift 5.12c★★★ (143)
☐ Vision Quest 5.12d★★ (130)

Climbs by Name

MORE FROM SUPERTOPO

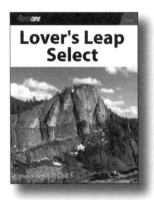

LAKE TAHOE'S CLIMBING GEM
LOVERS LEAP SELECT (eBook)
List Price: $9.95 Available at www.supertopo.com

This guide includes virtually all the moderate classic routes at Lover's Leap. Most of these climbs are well-protected, two to four pitches long, and ascend the incredible granite that Lover's Leap is known for. Because these routes have so many face holds and good rests, they are the perfect introduction to granite trad climbing and outdoor climbing in general.

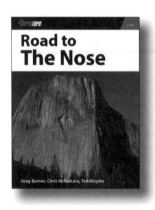

EVER WANTED TO CLIMB A BIG WALL?
ROAD TO THE NOSE (eBook)
List Price: $14.95 Available at www.supertopo.com

Many climbers consider The Nose of El Capitan the crowning achievement of a climbing career. In the *Road to The Nose*, big wall master Chris McNamara takes you through 14 climbs of increasing difficulty to help you build skills, speed, endurance, and comfort with big wall climbing. This guide includes special tips and beta specific to The Nose as well as more general information on getting ready for your first big wall.

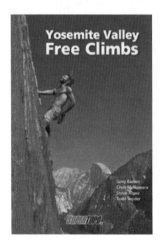

THE BEST TOPOS FOR YOSEMITE'S BEST CLIMBS
YOSEMITE VALLEY FREE CLIMBS (Print Book)
List Price: $29.95 Available at www.supertopo.com

This guidebook includes over 230 of the best routes in Yosemite Valley from 16-pitch trad climbs to one-pitch sport routes. While many hard Yosemite testpieces are included, this book focuses on topropes, crags, and multi-pitch climbs in the 5.4-5.9 range. We also include formerly obscure climbs to provide more options for avoiding crowds. As in all SuperTopo books, the authors personally climbed and documented each route with meticulous care to create the most detailed and accurate topos ever published.

MORE FROM SUPERTOPO

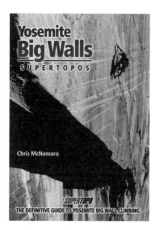

UNPRECEDENTED BIG WALL BETA
YOSEMITE BIG WALLS (Print Book)
List Price: $29.95 Available at www.supertopo.com

Written by Chris McNamara who personally climbed
and painstakingly documented every route, this book
includes essential route details such as climbing strategy,
retreat information, descent topos, pitch lengths, and
gear recommendations for each pitch. Yosemite Big Walls
covers the 41 best big wall routes on El Capitan, Half
Dome, Washington Column, and Leaning Tower.

OUTSTANDING PEAKS AND DOMES IN THE HIGH SIERRA
TUOLUMNE FREE CLIMBS (Print Book)
List Price: $24.95 Available at www.supertopo.com

Tuolumne Free Climbs includes over 110 of the best routes
in Tuolumne Meadows from 14-pitch trad climbs to one-
pitch sport routes. This book focuses on topropes, crags,
and multi-pitch climbs in the 5.4-5.9 range. Includes
formerly obscure climbs to provide more options for
avoiding crowds. As in all SuperTopo books, the authors
personally climbed and documented each climb with
meticulous care to create the most detailed and accurate
topos ever published.

ALPINE ROCK CLIMBING PARADISE
HIGH SIERRA SELECT (eBook)
List Price: $14.95 Available at www.supertopo.com

Included here are 14 classic High Sierra rock climbs
ranging in difficulty from 3rd class to 5.10b. Most of these
are well-protected, 10 to 15 pitches long, and ascend some
of the best alpine granite anywhere. Whether you plan to
scramble up the 3rd class East Ridge of Mt. Russell, climb
the 5.7 East Face of Mt. Whitney, or ascend the epic 18-
pitch Sun Ribbon Arête, this guidebook will ensure you
spend minimum time getting off route and maximum
time enjoying the climbing.

About the Authors

Greg Barnes

Greg has been climbing since 1994, and he can tell you every move on every route he's done, draw a topo from memory, give you his opinion on the rating of any pitch, repeat anything written in any guidebook, and tell you about the weather that day. He is Director of the American Safe Climbing Association. Between March 2001 and November 2002, Greg spearheaded the replacement of 482 bolts in Red Rocks canyons, including most of the long routes in this guidebook. He and other ASCA volunteers work long and hard to restore deteriorating bolts. Please support the ASCA by visiting www.safeclimbing.org and donating! Greg lives in Bishop, Yosemite, Tuolumne, Joshua Tree, and Red Rocks and develops SuperTopos for these areas.

Larry DeAngelo

Larry started climbing way back in 1969 in Southern California. Stony Point, Tahquitz, and the Southern Sierra were home back then. He moved to Las Vegas in late 1980s and Red Rocks is home now. Due to a serious inclination to live in the past, history comes naturally to Larry. His anachronistic approach (he still ties in with a swami belt and uses a hip belay) has caused some of the local climbers to grace him with the nickname "Scary Larry." He wears it as a badge of honor, since the sound of it suggests a reputation for boldness that he feels unlikely to earn based on climbing skill. His day-to-day profession is writing business software and consulting.

The Final Pitch

Chris McNamara

Thanks for buying this SuperTopo guidebook. We hope you enjoy it and the climbing adventure it may help you experience.

Your purchase means a lot to us. We here at SuperTopo are climbers who have set out to create a small business dedicated to giving you, and climbers like you, immediate access to the kind of detailed information you can normally only get by talking with a local expert. It takes a lot of work to create each SuperTopo and we're committed to making sure it's done right.

We're on a mission to develop SuperTopos for the best routes in the best climbing areas in North America. We hold ourselves strictly accountable to a high standard, namely that each of our SuperTopos offers the very finest quality route information obtainable anywhere on each and every route we cover. If you find any shortcoming in our SuperTopos, we ask that you drop us a line at: feedback@supertopo.com and let us know how we can improve. We're dedicated to offering the best information about every route available.

If you found this SuperTopo guidebook useful, we'd like to ask you two favors:

- Please post a message about your experience climbing these routes for the benefit of other climbers at: www.supertopo.com/routebeta

- Tell your friends about SuperTopo. We're about as "grassroots" an organization as you can imagine, and are entirely dependent on word-of-mouth referrals to keep producing quality SuperTopos.

On behalf of myself and the rest of the crew here at SuperTopo, I want to thank you for your support. Keep climbing and please tell a friend about SuperTopo!

Thanks again,

Chris McNamara

Founder and CEO
SuperTopo